BEYOND THE RED CARPET

HOW TO BECOME A

CORPORATE FLIGHT ATTENDANT

ON A PRIVATE JET

By

GAIL HOPKE

ISBN: 0-75961-360-5

This book is printed on acid free paper.

1stBooks - rev. 01/25/01

DEDICATION

This book is dedicated to all those who supported and encouraged my incredible dream of stepping beyond life's realities into a world of excellence that others had established before me; and to my wonderful husband, Ken, who still makes my life an incredible journey, beyond the red carpet.

PREFACE

While working as a corporate flight attendant I was often approached by people asking me how I acquired such a unique job. They were curious as to what type of extraordinary skills and talents I must have had in order to be traveling around the world in luxurious private jets, attending to the rich and famous, and getting paid to do it. When they learned that they too could meet the requirements with a little effort on their part, it inspired their great interest. While searching for reference materials to help them I found that although there was an abundance of information available for airline flight attendants, there was very little for corporate flight attendants. It seemed that unless one were involved in corporate aviation or had friends who worked in the business, obtaining corporate flight attendant information was difficult. My decision to write this book was a direct result of this.

This book is designed to be used as a supplement to the formal instruction provided at established cabin-crew-training facilities. Each chapter is designed to give you the basic knowledge required for this job and to help maximize your potential for employment as a corporate flight attendant, once you are formally trained. Once hired, you will be in a unique job unlike any other in the world. So, if you have a great love of people, places and planes, and a fierce determination to uphold the dedication and commitment that are required within this profession, then turn the pages and let your journey beyond the red-carpeted world of corporate aviation begin.

INTRODUCTION

"Two minutes" called out the Secret Service agent as he repositioned the earphone in his ear. At that command the captain, copilot and I gave our uniforms the once over and hurried down the stairs of our jet to meet the motorcade containing our passengers – a former U.S. President and First Lady. As I waited for the motorcade to arrive I couldn't help but feel that I had to be one of the luckiest persons alive. I had always wanted to be part of an aviation team in one way or another, but never thought it would be quite like this. Bypassing years of airline ranks I had made it into "big time" corporate aviation, the first time. Why was this so incredible? To begin with I was overweight (for airline standards), over forty years of age, a foreigner, and I had never worked formerly in aviation before.

A few years earlier I had come to the end of a low-paid, dismal job and at that stage I really couldn't say that I had any exceptional talents except that I loved the three "P's" – people, places and planes. I felt there had to be a new and better life beyond the confines of the orange carpeted floors of my six by five office cubicle. I yearned to be free of the ticking time clock, the weekly reports and the constant surveillance of a boss who really didn't seem to appreciate the great work I felt I was doing. It was time for a change!

"Good morning, Gail," came the robust voice of the former President as he alighted from his limousine. "Good morning, Mr. President," came my reply as I reached out eagerly to assist him with his luggage.

My career path had indeed changed its course! Now my office was the world, my time clock was Zulu and my carpets were now red. I had entered the exciting, glamorous, wonderful world of corporate aviation; a world that was only obtainable by reaching beyond the apparently impossible. This could be you!

CONTENTS

PART ONE:
THE CORPORATE FLIGHT ATTENDANT

CHAPTER 1: THE BASIC JOB DESCRIPTION

The job of a corporate flight attendant is quite unique. Depending on the company you go to work for and the FAA regulations, for example, Part 91, or Part 135, that they operate under, your duties and responsibilities can vary greatly. There are no set rules governing this position, as long as you are trained in the required FAA emergency procedures. Don't be fooled though into thinking that no other training is needed as, with any other job, there may be plenty of well-trained people eager for the same position if you fail to meet the necessary standards.

The following is a list of basic duties and responsibilities that you could expect when hired. Not all of these will be required and there may be many more that are not included; however, this will help you to determine whether or not you feel you have the "right stuff" to become a corporate flight attendant.

- **HAVE A GENUINE DESIRE AND WILLINGNESS TO SERVE OTHERS**
  This is one area you can't fake, especially when you're jet-lagged. You must possess emotional maturity and an even temperament, not given to wide mood swings or depression. It's not unusual for you to be in Los Angeles for breakfast, New York for lunch and London for dinner - all in one day! There will probably be little time to sit down and rarely any time to nap, even if it is allowed. Your true willingness to serve others will soon become apparent, especially when you're tired. Remember, if a dispute arises you cannot storm outside at 45,000 feet!

- **BE FREE TO TRAVEL WORLDWIDE, OFTEN AT A MOMENT'S NOTICE**
  You should be able to travel without a prearranged schedule, stay away from home for weeks at a time, if necessary, and work extended hours - often at a moment's notice. (If you have a family, or other personal commitments, this may mean hiring live-in help or a personal assistant.)

- **BE ABLE TO COMPLETE INITIAL AND RECURRENT CREW-MEMBER TRAINING**
  Your training will include all areas of emergency procedures. You will be required to climb in and out of small porthole windows in a simulated smoked-filled environment of an aircraft, as well as haul yourself and your "passengers" into life rafts, bobbing around in choppy waters. The last procedure requires considerable strength so being physically fit and composed under pressure are obviously essential.

  Although corporations are more lenient than airlines regarding physical attributes, it's best to ensure that you are basically in shape and that your weight is in proportion to your height. Age is not really a factor, either, as long as you can complete your training. This means you can be over fifty and still get hired! Don't despair if you feel you are beyond the limits. If you really have a burning desire to become a corporate flight attendant then getting into shape will be a choice, not a chore.

- **KNOW ALL NATIONAL AND INTERNATIONAL AVIATION PROCEDURES**
  This will require that you have a thorough knowledge in all aspects of local and international aviation operations and procedures, as well as the FAA (Federal Aviation Administration) rules and regulations for safety and security.

- **PROVIDE FIRST-CLASS SERVICE TO ALL PASSENGERS AND CREW**
  Your passengers may include royalty, politicians, film and television stars, along with company executives, their family and friends. It is important that you know the correct forms of address and the do's and don'ts associated with each individual's culture and lifestyle. Many of your passengers will look upon the plane as their refuge from the prying world of press, photographers and fans. You must ensure that their rights of privacy are met, even when they are sitting only three feet away. Everyone on board should be given first-class service, whether they are high profile or not. This also

includes the rest of the flight crew - especially the pilots. Remember, if the pilots don't make it, you probably won't, either.

- **MAINTAIN SOLE LEADERSHIP RESPONSIBILITY UNDER THE DIRECTION OF THE PILOT-IN-COMMAND**

    Most corporate jets require only one flight attendant. This means that you could assume multiple roles as chef, hostess, nanny, official greeter, cleaner, secretary, travel agent and more. The important point to remember is that whatever role you are called to do, you must be good at it. When you're around the other side of the world the passengers (and sometimes the crew), will often rely on you as their sole source for assistance. Above-average leadership skills and the ability to make sound decisions are absolutely necessary.

    Perhaps the most important aspect of all is your ability to maintain confidentiality. Nothing you see, hear, or experience with your passengers is to be repeated without their permission – ever! Remember, when the journey's long over, it's your passengers who will be your final reference.

- **BE ABLE TO PLAN, PURCHASE, PREPARE AND SERVE GOURMET MEALS**

    In most cases you will be responsible for catering to each passenger's individual needs regarding food service and ensuring that it meets the required health standards at all times. You may be responsible for the budget as well, which can be quite challenging when you are preparing expensive gourmet food on a limited income. Your creative abilities in catering will be quickly noticed when you travel to third-world countries where the word "gourmet" is non existent. Of course, not all corporate aircraft have gourmet service, in fact, some don't have any food service at all. This book, though, will help prepare you for the ultimate and the most challenging aspects of gourmet in-flight food service that you will prepare and serve from a galley only slightly larger than a broom closet.

- **BE ABLE TO DECORATE OR MAINTAIN THE AMBIANCE OF A PLANE'S INTERIOR BEFITTING THE COMPANY IMAGE**

    Each company has its own requirements for what they feel constitutes their image of ambiance. It will be your responsibility to find out what your company's preference is. This area includes lighting, food and beverages, entertainment such as music, videos, and whatever else they consider to be important. Once you know what their preferences are, make sure you adhere to them. Your personal opinions are probably the wrong opinions, no matter how right they may seem to you, as the customer is right in this situation.

- **BE ABLE TO ADJUST TO THIRD-WORLD ENVIRONMENTS**

    If you're the type who likes to camp out and rough it occasionally or you have a survivor mentality, then you will probably be better able to cope with the lack of conveniences and human deprivation associated with some of the third-world countries. It's not unusual for "hotels" in these environments to suffer from food and water shortages, poor sanitation or be without heat and air-conditioning, despite the extremes in weather. Having maturity, compassion and great love for humanity, no matter what their circumstances, may help you enjoy a long career as a corporate flight attendant. There is definitely no room for self-centeredness, hardened hearts, or egotists in this profession.

- **HELP ENSURE BAGGAGE IS LOADED AND UNLOADED AND SAFELY TRANSPORTED BETWEEN HOTELS AND AIRPORTS, IF NECESSARY**

    Usually the pilots, flight engineer, or the airport ground handlers take care of the loading and unloading of baggage to and from an aircraft, but be prepared to do this, as well as personally delivering the passengers' baggage to their rooms. Make sure you ask about baggage responsibilities during your interview before you end up jet-lagged, fourteen hours later around the other side of the world in a country where there is no valet service, no elevators and five stories of broken, narrow, concrete stairs to maneuver your way up.

- **BE ABLE TO MAINTAIN AIRCRAFT INVENTORY SYSTEMS AND SUPPLIES**
    You will be required to maintain updated Inventory and Supplies Lists ensuring that they meet the requirements for the hectic pace that most corporate flight departments seem to work under. This will include stocking food, beverages and emergency supplies prior to flight and knowing how to use them. In some countries food, water and medicines are not always available, so it is vital that you have the correct supplies on board appropriate to the country you are traveling to. Replenishing all supplies at the end of a journey is therefore absolutely essential.

- **MAINTAIN A CURRENT "SQUAWKS" (CABIN REPAIR) LIST**
    Before and after each flight it is necessary to check the entire internal area of the plane including the cabin, galley, lavatory, baggage, as well as all safety equipment. You must know how to inspect seats, lights, entertainment systems, telephones and other accessories, for proper operation and to keep a current "squawks" list for anything that needs repair or service. This list is to be given to the Pilot-In-Command at the end of each flight. Before the commencement of a new flight, you must check the items listed and ensure that they have been repaired or serviced, before you travel.

- **BE ABLE TO CLEAN THE AIRCRAFT INTERIOR**
    Private jets are often lavishly outfitted with the finest of fabrics and furnishings ranging from marble bathrooms to suede ceilings and solid gold accessories. Add to this the fine china, crystal stemware and exquisite cutlery service, and you have a situation where one mishap could cost thousands of dollars to repair or replace. It is essential that you know how to clean the interior and that you have the right cleaning equipment to do the job properly, as professional help will not always be available. This will most likely require your getting some instruction from the professionals themselves.

- **ENSURE THAT YOUR UNIFORM IS SPOTLESS AND THAT PROPER IDENTIFICATION IS WORN WHILE WORKING**
    If you are assigned a uniform to wear then it should look immaculate when it's worn. Always remember that you are a reflection of the company you work for and when you greet your passengers, you are often the first person from your company they will meet. They may scrutinize you carefully to see what sort of image your company allows their employees to project. Any identification, such as a name and photo badge, should be clearly visible so that passengers, airport officials and others, know whom they are addressing and from which aircraft you are.

- **OTHER DUTIES AS ASSIGNED**
    As it was mentioned under the leadership responsibility section you will find that duty requirements can vary greatly within each flight department. One company may expect their flight attendant to become the nanny to children aboard a ship or yacht once the flight destination has been reached. Another company may expect their flight attendant to assume the role of travel agent or secretary to any passengers once they have landed, while another company may leave you completely alone to enjoy your days of rest. There are no set guidelines except those agreed upon at your initial interview.
    It's obvious from the above that you will need to determine your energy and social levels before you make a commitment to a flight attendant position within a company. Finding out what the "other duties as assigned" are, can mean the difference between keeping or losing your job or "jobs." Remember, if you get fired from one it will be difficult finding another in such a competitive, exclusive world where excellence of service is always expected to be maintained.

Once you accept a position within a company remember that it takes an extraordinary team effort to make each flight a success and it's usually the flight attendant who sets the pace, because he, or she, is constantly visible to those who are being served. The message is quite clear– set the right pace and you will be walking beyond the red carpet, for a long, long time.

CHAPTER 2: GETTING THE RIGHT TRAINING

Most corporations prefer flight attendants who are trained before they commence employment although there are a few who have been hired and trained from within a company's structure. As there are an abundance of flight attendants in comparison to available positions, it is strongly advisable that you gain as much knowledge and education as possible, especially when starting out.

There are four different FAA structures that a corporate flight attendant can be hired under. They are called Federal Aviation Regulations (FARs) Part 91, Part 121, Part 125 and Part 135. Each category is based on the type of plane, such as cargo or passenger, and the type of flying the company will be doing, such as domestic, international, private or commercial. Most of you, however, will be flying under Part 91 or Part 135.

Part 91 does not require any specific training except that a crew member must be able to prove to the Pilot-In-Command that they can operate the emergency equipment on board the aircraft and evacuate passengers in an emergency. For this very reason, it is highly recommended that you obtain formal training.

Part 135, however, requires that all crew members complete FAA-approved emergency training. Training will include instruction on most of the following:

- Aerospace physiology
- Aircraft emergency equipment
- Cockpit/cabin fire and smoke situations
- Emergency evacuations from your aircraft including procedures in wet ditching
- FARs (Federal Aviation Regulations)
- Hijackers, bomb threats and other unusual circumstances
- Identification of hazardous materials
- Medical emergencies
- Passenger briefings
- Water survival

There are a number of excellent crew training facilities in the USA with most of them providing the minimum Part 135 requirements. Listed below are some of the main ones:

FACTS TRAINING INTERNATIONAL
3633 81ST Ave., SW
Olympia, WA 98512, USA

TEL: 360-754-9805
FAX: 360-754-1911
www.facts-aircare.com

STARK SURVIVAL
6227 E. HWY., 98
Panama City,
FL 32404, USA

TEL: 850-871-4730
FAX:850-871-0668
www.starksurvival.com

FLIGHT SAFETY INTERNATIONAL
Cabin Attendant Training
301 Robert B. Miller Rd.
Savannah, GA 31408, USA

TEL: 800-625-9369
www.flightsafety.com

FLIGHT SAFETY INTERNATIONAL
Cabin Attendant Training
1804 Hyannis Court
Atlanta, GA 30337, USA

TEL: 800-889-7916
www.flightsafety.com

Fees for basic flight attendant training can range from $1500 - $5000. You must also include additional fees for extra classes, plus travel and lodging if necessary. Some training companies travel around the USA teaching at various facilities, so call first to see if there's one close to where you live to avoid these additional costs. While the prices may seem steep, remember that as far as most careers go, it's cheap! Many jobs require that you have a degree, which costs considerably more to get, and that you have prior experience before you're hired. In corporate aviation a degree and prior experience, although desirable, are generally not a requirement. This makes it advantageous for anyone who desires to be a corporate flight attendant to be able to become one without spending many years in college. Perhaps the greatest savings of all is that you will be traveling the world first class and getting paid to do it. This means your very first trip will probably cover all your costs of training. It doesn't get much better than that!

OPTIONAL EXTRAS

These extras are not required; however, you may wish to take them as a complement to your basic training. They represent valuable instruction that will not only help you on the job, but also in your personal life as well. Although I have listed only a few addresses you will find that many of them are located around America and can even be taken by distance learning or correspondence as well. They are a great way to fill in those long hours while waiting for your passengers around the airport ramps of the world.

MEDICAL:

Given the increase in bloodborne pathogens such as Immunodeficiency disease (HIV) and Hepatitis B (HBV), it is highly recommended that you take extra classes in addition to your basic training, and even more so if these are not covered. It is also recommended that you learn how to use the automatic external defibrillator (AED) to assist in cardiac emergencies as well. An excellent sources for medical training is:

MEDAIRE, INC
1301 E. McDowell Rd.
Suite 204
Phoenix, AZ 85006, USA

TEL: 602-452-4300
FAX: 602-252-8404
www.medaire.com

On an airline with lots of passengers there's a good chance that someone is skilled in the medical field; however, on a private jet with few passengers these odds are greatly reduced, so it just makes sense to learn as much as you can to be better prepared for any emergency.

FOOD SERVICE:

One of the most important aspects of your job will be the presentation of meals served in an appetizing and appealing manner. While you don't need to become a chef or a caterer to do this, it would help to have some extra training in the art of preparing and presenting food in a gourmet style. The larger, private jets fly at higher altitudes where the air is calmer and therefore, this makes it conducive to using fine china and crystal. How much nicer then if the flight attendant knows how to serve a meal that's not only cooked to perfection, but is presented in such a way that it adds a luxurious touch complementing everything around it. It's not difficult to do this; in fact, most flight attendants will tell you it just takes only a little instruction to make a plate look like something out of the Ritz! The key is artistry in preparing the food and the use of garnishments to add beauty.

Most training facilities offer extra classes in food service and preparation and you are strongly urged to take them. While they may be rather basic courses, they will teach you safety factors of serving food and pouring beverages while working in cramped quarters of a moving aircraft. You may also want to hone your skills by taking some external classes as ongoing continuing education. Believe me, the pleasure and excitement expressed by passengers when they see the feast you have prepared for them is well with the effort.

Fortunately, culinary arts is a thriving industry in America, so finding a place to get some hands-on experience near your home is not that difficult. There are numerous ways to learn so find one that fits in with your schedule. Don't overlook the local restaurants for ideas, junior colleges for classes, or various food and wine courses that always seem to be advertised. Just in case you want to go further I have included a sample of some formal establishments that will take you to the ultimate heights in the food industry and perhaps in your aviation career as well.

THE CULINARY INSTITUTE OF AMERICA
1946 Campus Drive
Hyde Park, NY 12538, USA
TEL: 845-452-9600
www.ciachef.edu

JNA INSTITUTE OF CULINARY ARTS
1212 South Broad Street,
Philadelphia, PA 19146, USA
TEL: 215-468-8800
www.culinaryarts.com

ORAL COMMUNICATION:

Proper speech and diction are two very important attributes you must master in this work. You will need to be able to communicate with dignitaries, heads of state, royalty and others in a confident and professional manner. If your speech is full of slang, colloquialisms or current buzzwords, then it's recommended that you learn how to overcome these traits or habits. Some of you may have perfect communication skills but lack the confidence of speaking in public or to those in authority. Fortunately, there are numerous ways for you to develop these strengths and help get you striding confidently, beyond the red carpet.

For classes in speech there are two excellent sources you can choose from that are inexpensive and extremely valuable in what they have to offer.

JUNIOR COLLEGES
Located nation wide - consult the telephone Yellow Pages for one near you.
Look for "Speech 101" or something similar.
(Contact an academic counselor if necessary.)

TOASTMASTERS INTERNATIONAL
P.O. Box 9052
Mission Viejo, CA 92690, USA

TOASTMASTERSINTERNATIONAL
23182 Arroyo Vista
Rancho Santa Margarita,
CA 92688, USA

TEL: 949-858-8255
FAX: 949-858-1207
www.toastmasters.org

Do not consider taking these classes online because you need the support of your classmates and the feedback from the instructor to get you to maximum speaking performance. A key advantage also is that you get to learn from watching others in your class gain the skills to become proficient speakers.

If you want to know how you look now, take a video of yourself giving a speech presentation and when you have completed your training, take another. I'm sure you will agree there is a magnitude of difference for the better. Don't be depressed if your first taping is poor, just remember that even those great broadcasters you watch on television have all gone through many hours of training, so you're not alone in your quest.

PILOT/AVIATION GROUND SCHOOL:

Finally, you may also want to learn the basics in piloting skills without the hassle of learning how to fly, unless of course you want to. This can be achieved by taking an Aviation Ground School course that covers aerodynamics, weather, navigation and more. Not only will you greatly benefit from this knowledge, but it will also provide a certain amount of reassurance for your passengers, especially the fearful flyers, when they realize your knowledge goes beyond the interior of an aircraft cabin. Your pilot teammates will also appreciate your ability to comprehend the basics of their job so anyway you look at it, everybody wins! A popular trend these days seems to be for pilots and flight engineers to cross-train as flight attendants, so why should you not try to do the same; besides, you might be surprised at just how far you advance.

Ground school classes are readily available at most airports around the country. Some training centers also offer the ground school portion via distance learning and this is quite acceptable for what you want to do. If you can spend a few extra dollars you may want to go up in a small plane with an instructor and actually experience the thrill of flight as a pilot. The least it will do for you is enhance your love of flying and aviation beyond your wildest imagination.

Some good sources for aviation instruction include:

AMERICAN FLYERS
(Numerous locations throughout America – call for location nearest you)
TEL: 800-362-0808
www.americanflyers.net

OR

AMERICAN FLYERS
(INTERNATIONAL INQUIRIES)
TEL: 954-785-1450
FAX: 954-784-2128
www.af-usa@msn.com

WINGS INTERNATIONAL
2635 Cunningham Ave.,
San Jose, CA 95148, USA
TEL: (001)-408-251-6085
FAX: (001) 408-251-8919
www.wingsinternational.com

FIND A FLIGHT SCHOOL
www.findaflightschool.com

By following the basic guidelines in this chapter you should be well on your way to one of the most exciting careers in the world. As mentioned earlier, it doesn't require a college degree or years of training; in fact, you could be finished with all your classes in as little as two months. Of course that would take great dedication and determination, but after all, that's what being a corporate flight attendant requires.

CHAPTER 3: PROJECTING A PROFESSIONAL IMAGE

Once hired you will be projecting the company image in a very public way. Often, you are the first company representative passengers will meet and so how you present yourself will have a lasting impression. Because of this we are going to assume in this chapter that you have had little or no experience in any type of up-scale, high-profile or professional environment. The rules are simple, but if you don't know them, your efforts to look professional may be futile. This chapter then will help give you that edge to create a winning look.

Most companies want their crew in some sort of uniform. Those that don't still want you to represent them in a professional way. A key point to remember is that when you travel overseas you will often stay in the same hotel as the passengers (and perhaps your boss), because the hotel you're staying in may be the only one in town. You may raise a few eyebrows when you appear on the plane as a professional person and the following morning, turn up for breakfast looking totally bedraggled! Once you're home and away from the job then you can do what you like; however, while you are traveling and working on company time, and that includes, unfortunately, your "free" time in many cases, you should continue to maintain a professional image. Just because the boss and passengers may arrive dressed like slobs doesn't mean that you can, too.

Always try to keep that professionalism. Remember, other flight crews may be watching you on one of the many terminal ramps around the world and if you decide to lower your standards temporarily, one of them may be your future boss!

The following will help in assisting you to achieve that professional look.

WOMEN

THE IDEAL FIGURE

The first thing you must do is to determine your body shape and size. If your body proportions appear to be "out of alignment" then go to a health club, hire a personal trainer or visit a doctor to see what can be done. Through applying a diet and exercise routine on a regular basis you can obtain the results you desire. Don't be too critical with yourself because the great majority of women believe that they fit into the "out-of alignment" category, so you're not alone.

Once you have decided on a health maintenance plan, visit a fashion consultant at an established store and learn how to wear clothes that look best on you. The right clothing style can give the appearance of adding or reducing your height and weight, so invest in this time because the results will be worth it.

SUITS AND DRESSES

For a professional look **suits and dresses** should be conservative. While a leather-clad pant suit and a Spanish flamenco dress may make you the belle of the party, it's best to leave them at home. Instead, opt for plain colors in shades of navy, tan, black or white and made in natural fabrics such as wool, cotton or silk. Accessorize the plain outfits with colorful scarves, hats and jewelry. Hem lengths should be close to the knee. Although fashion may dictate thigh-high thrillers, remember it was the conservative, glamorous look that rocketed Princess Diana and Jackie Kennedy to the front pages of the glamour magazines decades apart.

JACKETS AND JEANS

Jackets should be conservative and rather plain in pattern and color, also. It's a good idea to have a number of them so that you can mix and match them with clothes in your wardrobe. Once again, natural fibers work best and when a jacket is worn over a dress or jeans (no holes please!), it helps to give that chic look. When wearing pants or **jeans**, forget the "attractively tight" look. Clothing must enhance the body, not restrict it. An important point to remember is that your body expands at altitude, sometimes up to an inch, which may mean your attractively tight jeans may become uncomfortably tight.

SHIRTS AND BLOUSES

These should be in cotton or washable silk and complement you as well as the outfits you are wearing. Avoid synthetic materials such as polyester or rayon. While they may look great on, in hot, humid weather the fabric causes you to perspire extensively and so should be avoided completely.

HOSIERY

One of the most important points to remember with hosiery is to never wear them with a run or hole in them. This will cheapen your image and give the impression that you are negligent in your personal attire. Of course mishaps will happen, but be prepared and always carry a spare pair in your purse or luggage.

It's best to wear tan, black or white nylons and perhaps navy blue with your uniform, but you are well advised to avoid the fishnet styles as well as those that have the thick reinforced toes and heels, which detract from your overall appearance.

UNDERWEAR

Underwear should be worn but never seen. Throw away bras they have twisted mangled straps, fraying fibers or are loose and hang down from your shoulders. For overseas flying it is best to stay with the more durable, natural fabric of cotton. The finer fabrics such as silk and satin made in delicate styles with a lot of lace do not last long in the harsh waters of many overseas countries.

SHOES, BAGS AND SCARVES

Shoes and handbags should be in plain colored leather and match. The best shoes to buy are leather pumps, or flats, as they can be worn with almost anything and are comfortable to wear. Always make sure they are polished and in good condition, being free from holes, tears and scuff marks.

Handbags should be large enough to carry all your personal items. An adjustable shoulder strap will come in handy when you juggle passport, visa and luggage at an airport check-in counter. Leather is sturdier and will tolerate a lot more weight and will not tear or rip as easily as the vinyl or fake leathers.

Scarves are the greatest accessories. By learning how to twist and tie them into various shapes and sizes you can visually change the same outfit into a multitude of styles for any occasion. You can wear them around your neck, around the waist, across the shoulders, in your hair or even tied to your handbag. Washable silk is the easiest to work with and today they are inexpensive to buy, so make sure you buy lots of them to add color to your plainer outfits.

JEWELRY

It's a good idea when traveling to leave your valuables at home as there really is no safe place to keep them. If you must take jewelry and are worried about loss then get a jeweler to make replicas and take those with you instead, but don't forget the golden rule - least is best. Too much jewelry looks trashy, likewise cheap jewelry; however, wedding and engagement rings (no matter how cheap), along with a nice watch are quite acceptable. Earrings should be limited to one per ear and they should preferably be in gold or good quality silver. Pearls, diamonds, even good quality simulated stones are also very acceptable. Avoid earrings that have large loops or spikes that may cause damage or injury to yourself and others.

It's also a good idea to invest in a waterproof, dual-time watch so that you can keep track of the times, both at home and at your present or intended location. There will probably be many occasions when you will need to call home or the office and knowing the time there may mean a great deal to your professional and personal future. Incidentally, one of the most asked questions by passengers is for the time at home and the intended destination.

HAIR, NAILS AND MAKEUP

You must learn how to do your **hair** yourself. If it's long, learn how to put it up or tie it back using some of the hair accessories that are available on the market today. Ask your hairdresser to give you a style that will be easy to manage. If you happen to be traveling through the Amazon jungle or Australia's Northern Territory you will soon come to realize that it's a long way to a beauty salon. For the same reason you should also learn how to do your own **nails**. Stores now sell great nail kits suitable for traveling, so try some out and see what works best for you.

Just as there are many types of faces there are many types of **makeup**. What looks good on one person can be a disaster on another. If you're uncertain as to what suits you then visit your local beauty counter and ask for a facial. Usually these facials are free. This way you will be able to experiment with a variety of cosmetics and find the ones that flatter you without wasting money.

As a guide you will need some moisturized foundation to cope with the dry cabin air, soft colored eyeshadow, lipstick and waterproof mascara. Many of the makeup foundations and lipsticks now include a sunscreen, which is beneficial for additional outdoor protection. Buy these if you can.

PERSONAL HYGIENE

Your teeth should be white and without any visible defects. Braces are quite acceptable, but broken or missing teeth, especially in the front, are definitely not. A trip to the dentist to repair these could make or break your potential career. If halitosis is a problem either see your dentist or carry some mints in your pocket and remember to use them. Never chew gum or tobacco.

You must shower or bathe every day - there is no exception to the rule! Avoid using perfumes, sprays and colognes because in a compact cabin environment the aroma could make passengers sick. Body hair under the arms and legs (and maybe the face) should be removed. It may be acceptable for women to be hairy in some cultures, but in our western culture it is not. If hair removal is difficult for you then you should consider permanent removal, which can be done in a beauty salon. It may cost a little more, but remember that if it's done right it needs to be done only once.

MEN

THE IDEAL SHAPE

For some unknown reason men don't seem to fuss over their bodies as much as women, perhaps because they don't have as many problems with fat storage and disposal. Regardless, some of you do and so you are also advised to consult a doctor, visit a health club or hire a personal trainer.

NOTE: One area many men seem to need help in the most is in fashion coordination. If you're uncertain how to get that dressed-for-success look then visit a quality men's wear store and ask advice from a skilled salesperson. They're seldom wrong.

SUITS

The important point is to buy quality. Nothing takes away from a professional image more than a shabby, crumpled suit hanging limply on your body. It doesn't have to be expensive – just look it. Natural fibers such as wool, silk and tweed will hold their shape longer than synthetics. The patterns should be plain and in conservative colors such as charcoal, navy or gray. Avoid the outdated checkered patterns of the fifties and the wide-striped (except pinstripes) ones of the sixties. Make sure the trouser legs are long enough to cover the tops of your shoes and the jacket sleeves are long enough to extend over your wrists. Remember, the Peewee Herman look is out!

JACKETS AND JEANS

You should own a couple of sports jackets and, once again, they should be in natural fibers. Linen, however, may look great but should be avoided as it creases easily and is therefore not suitable for travel. Jeans can be in any color, but leave all those with holes in them at home.

SHIRTS, TIES AND BELTS

The best **shirts** for traveling in are drip-dry cotton. They should be starched and pressed with all the buttons attached. Large checkered patterns and wide stripes are rather outdated, so it's preferable to avoid them. Avoid bright, bold colors such as purple, pink and orange, which look great in the tropics, but could draw too much attention to you in poorer or crime-ridden countries. White is always a winner and blends in with everything.

When you buy a **tie** make sure it is of the finest quality, blends in with the colors you are wearing and is long enough to reach your belt. Don't wear a cravat or bow tie unless it's part of the company policy, required for a formal occasion or it's what the locals wear. Once again, the idea is not to draw attention to yourself or others who may be with you. Safety and security should always be your prime concern.

Belts should preferably be in plain black or brown leather and of a slim width. The buckles should be leather, gold or silver in color and make sure they are small. Keep those great looking cowboy buckles for working out on the ranch, or riding your Harley back home.

SHOES, SOCKS AND UNDERWEAR

Shoes should be in leather and in a standard color of black or brown. They should be highly polished and free of holes and scuff marks. It's a good idea to carry a traveler's shoe polish kit in your briefcase for those last-minute touchups. **Socks** should always be worn with suits and trousers no matter what the movie stars dictate, unless of course you're going to the beach. They should match your clothes and be long enough to cover visible leg under your trousers when you sit down.

Once again cotton is the best choice for **underwear** and is suitable for most climates. Make sure though that they look new as you will often have your luggage opened for customs inspections in full view of your fellow passengers and crew.

JEWELRY

Men's jewelry should be kept to an absolute minimum. Wedding bands, engagement rings, watches, aviation lapel pins and tie tacks are all acceptable, but it's best to leave your earrings, necklaces and bracelets at home where possible. The motto is "least is best."

PERSONAL HYGIENE

You must shower or bathe every day and there is no exception to the rule! Don't forget you are going to be sharing a tiny cabin area with a number of passengers and crew - possibly for hours. Your hair should be neatly trimmed, likewise your beard or mustache. If your hair is long then it should be brushed and tied back neatly.

Avoid fragrant aftershave lotions and deodorants as the aromas from these can be very distressing to airsick or allergic passengers. Your teeth should also be clean and white and without visible defects. Braces are acceptable, but broken or missing teeth, especially in the front, are not. Consult your dentist for immediate treatment if necessary. To combat halitosis, use breath mints but never chew gum or tobacco.

BRIEFCASES AND ACCESSORIES

A briefcase is highly visible, so buy the best. It should be preferably in a quality plain colored leather and it's okay to have your initials monogrammed on a corner, but leave the stickers and transfers for the kids' school bags. Avoid plastic or vinyl briefcases which not only look cheap, but also do not fare well in constant traveling. A synthetic material computer bag, however, is quite acceptable.

It's important to keep the briefcase interior tidy as it tends to reflect your personality when it's opened in public. A messy interior could mean that that's what you're like inside, too! Wallets should be thin enough to fit in your pocket without causing a bulge or, if necessary, place some of the contents in your briefcase and carry only the essentials.

GENERAL INFORMATION FOR MEN AND WOMEN

EXTRA ACCESSORIES

It's a good idea to invest in a **cellular phone** with voice mail attached. If necessary, get the vibrating type so that the ringing won't disturb those around you. A pager will also work, but sometimes it's difficult getting to a telephone to return the call, especially when you are traveling in an unknown area. When a trip is planned there will be many reasons for urgent communications such as catering questions, changes in the trip schedule, crew member questions, and so on. Also, if you are going to be working freelance then you must make sure you can be reached in a timely manner, otherwise the job may go to someone else.

Don't overlook a quality **pen and pencil set,** either, especially when it graces the inside pocket of your jacket or briefcase. Unless you can afford a high-quality pen, or one that looks as good as a Mont Blanc, avoid putting anything on display in a front pocket except perhaps a handkerchief. Also make sure that the pen you choose is able to withstand high altitude pressure. Many a crew member has experienced a pocket full of ink when not purchasing wisely.

FINE TUNING THAT ATTITUDE

Have you heard the expression "your attitude determines your latitude"? In this case it is true, literally and figuratively! Stop grumbling, complaining, back-biting, gossiping and all the other hideous traits that make yourself and others miserable. No one wants to be around a chronic loser and that's what you are if you keep up that negativity. STOP IT! By developing a heart of sharing and caring toward others you will find that most of your problems will simply disappear. Seek professional help if you feel your attitude's a problem and might stand in the way of your achieving the job of your dreams. In the long term you will enhance not only your life, but the lives of those around you.

The information above provides rather conservative guidelines for working in corporate aviation; however, you may work for a company that prefers something quite different. It is for this reason that you should research a company and the crew thoroughly before you commence employment, to see if you would fit in with their lifestyle. Always remember that no matter whether the company you go to work for is conservative or casual, you as their flight attendant must always project a confident, capable and professional image to be a success, and this success ultimately means that you will get beyond the red carpet for a long, long time.

CHAPTER 4: WRITING A WINNING RESUME

The next step in becoming a corporate flight attendant is to write a winning resume. There are many books and computer programs that can help you to do this, so it should not be too difficult. If you still feel perplexed, check the Yellow Pages of the telephone directory for a resume writing service. Their fees are usually very reasonable and their presentation of a high standard - an important factor in job hunting.

A basic resume guideline for a corporate flight attendant should include the following:

THE RESUME

- **HEADING**
  Write your full name, address, phone numbers including home, cellular and fax, and e-mail address if you have one.

- **OBJECTIVE**
  Mention that you want to become a corporate flight attendant.

- **EMPLOYMENT HISTORY**
  State the name and address of the company most recently worked at, giving the dates employed. Briefly describe your job description. List other jobs that you have worked over the last ten years in descending year order.

- **EDUCATION**
  Start with your highest qualification naming the institution and dates where the education was received. List any academic achievements obtained with each one.

- **SPECIAL TRAINING**
  List any other courses that you have successfully completed.

- **SPECIAL SKILLS**
  This may include language skills, travel experience, etc.

- **VOLUNTEER EXPERIENCE**
  List any volunteer experiences no matter how insignificant you may think they are.

- **MEMBERSHIPS**
  List any organizations that you are, or have been, involved in.

- **PERSONAL**
  List your general health, interests and availability for employment. Your age, weight, marital status and citizenship are optional.

- **REFERENCES**
  Make sure your references are available upon request. You may enclose copies with your resume when it's mailed.

It is important to keep your resume factual and within two pages. Use the best quality white paper and make sure that it is typed in standard type and free from errors. Always make sure you have extra copies with you during your job search or while on interviews.

SAMPLE RESUME

JAYNE JOHNSON
123 Smith Road
Cathedral City, CA 91604

24 hour (360) 234-XXXX/Mobile: (360) 987-XXXX
E-mail:jay@usa..XXX

OBJECTIVE: Acquire a corporate flight attendant position

EMPLOYMENT HISTORY:
Dec. 94-Present   RECEPTIONIST/SECRETARY
Global Travel Company, 1212 Main St., Los Angeles, CA. 92255
Secretary to five travel agents. Answer telephones and manage busy reception.
Experienced with Internet, Excel and Apollo ticketing.

Jan. 92-Dec. 94   BANQUET ASSISTANT
Sunlander Hotel, 121 Beach Blvd., Marina Del Rey, CA. 92245
Greet and seat approximately 250 guests per banquet function. Serve food and
beverages according to the hotel's fashionable image.

PART-TIME WORK:
(1990-Present)   FREELANCE FASHION MODEL
Bedford Model Agency, Pit St., Carson,
CA. 92260
Work as freelance model for a variety of department stores and special events.

EDUCATION:
Oct.-88   Associate Arts Degree – Psychology, (Dean's List: 3.74), West Lake University
1734 Plano Road, Los Angeles, CA. 92255

SPECIAL TRAINING:
Jan. 96   Certificate- First Aid/CPR, Red Cross, California
Dec. 95   Certificate - Flitestar Crew Training Academy, California
Aug. 95   Diploma – Jill's Food & Catering School, California
Aug. 89   Academy of Elegance Modeling School, California

VOLUNTEER WORK:
     Compare fashion shows for David Jones stores during festive seasons
     Volunteer fundraiser for the American Cancer Society

MEMBERSHIPS: Institute of Fashion Models of America

PERSONAL: Birthdate: May 28, 1970
Health: Excellent
Marital Status: Single –available to travel
Interests: Reading, photography, tennis, travel

REFERENCES: Available upon request

SAMPLE RESUME

JOHN WILLIAMSON
820 South Bay Road,
Corona, WA 98229

24 hour (390) 234-XXXX/Mobile: (390) 987-XXXX
E-mail:jws@nzws.XXX

OBJECTIVE:	Acquire a corporate flight attendant position

EMPLOYMENT HISTORY:

Aug. 96-Present   **ASSISTANT MANAGER**
Palms Hotel, Valley Springs, WA. 98230
Assist manager in all facets of hotel management including personnel, food and beverage services, administration etc.

July 91- Present   **REAL ESTATE AGENT**
Browns Realty Services, Corona, WA. 98229
Work evenings, weekends and public holidays.
List and sell residential homes in local area. Top salesperson for 1993.
Appeared on television as spokesperson for Realty Showcase.

July 87-July 91   **AIRPORT RAMP COORDINATOR**
Blaine Airport, Corona, WA. 98229
Responsible for refueling all types of aircraft from propellers planes to jets.
Assist passengers and flight-crew before takeoff and after arrival.
Also assist front desk clerk with invoicing and radio intercom service.

EDUCATION:
June 86   Bachelor of Arts – Business Administration.
(Valley College, Addington, WA. 98225)

SPECIAL TRAINING:
1997   Certificate: First Aid/CPR, Corona Hospital, Washington
1996   Certificate: Part 135/Part 91 Crew-member Training, Flight Tech, Washington
1993   Private Pilot's License, Washington
1991   Real Estate License, Washington

MEMBERSHIPS: Washington Pilot's Association
Toastmasters International

PERSONAL: Birthdate: 8/15/68
Health: Excellent
Interests: flying, running, golf, computers

REFERENCES: Available upon request

SAMPLE RESUME

Katie Bradford
15 Seddon St., Apt. 22
Dallas, TX 90049

24hr (569) 456-XXXX/Pager: (569) 662-XXXX

OBJECTIVE: To enter a full-time career as a corporate flight attendant

EMPLOYMENT HISTORY:

1997 – Present: PART-TIME WAITRESS
Mario's Italian Kitchen, 12344 Flowers Road., Dallas, TX, 90049
Responsible for serving approximately twenty-five tables, five evenings a week
in a very busy Italian restaurant. Presently being trained in food preparation and
beverages.

EDUCATION: Graduated Chandler High-School 1996 with honors

SPECIAL TRAINING: Certificate: First Aid/CPR – St. Patrick's Hospital, Dallas, Texas
Certificate: Flight Crew-Member training, Astroflite, Houston, Texas
Diploma: Travel Consultants of America, Dallas, Texas
Completed two years each of Spanish and Italian language

SPECIAL ACHIEVEMENTS:
Captain of Cheerleader team, Chandler High School, Dallas, Texas

VOLUNTEER WORK: Volunteered Saturday mornings at St. Patrick's Hospital, Dallas, Texas

PERSONAL: Birthdate: 10/15/79
Health: Excellent
Single: Available to travel worldwide
Interests: Aerobics, ski-ing, reading, cooking, travel

REFERENCES: Available upon request

Each of the three preceding resumes reflects training and/or involvement in different aspects associated with being a corporate flight attendant. It is strongly advisable that you have at least formal flight attending training before you begin your job search. It also helps if you can prove that you were a team leader, or could handle some significant responsibility prior to the interview. Unlike the airlines, corporate aviation personnel rarely work on a regular schedule and as a result, you also need to prove that you have in the past, kept up with a hectic, busy schedule, preferably handling multiple tasks at once, or have the ability to do so in the future.

THE COVER LETTER

With each resume mailed out you should enclose a cover letter that expresses your earnest desire to work for that company. This is your opportunity to catch the interviewer's attention and make them eager to read your resume because in it you will highlight all the reasons why they should hire you as their flight attendant. The body of your letter should be brief and to the point, and most of all, free of errors. You should also make sure that the cover letter you send out is on the same paper as your resume.

You should start off with your address, telephone, contact numbers and the date. You should also add the name of the company, their address and the contact person with all the information spelled correctly. After addressing the contact person summarize why you chose their company and why you want to work there. Do some research on the company and find out a few facts - this always attracts attention. An example would be to find out what areas of the world they fly to the most and why. Once you have this information you could make a quick study on that city or country because that's where you will most likely spend a lot of time. If the company flies frequently to the Middle East then you may want to study Muslim culture and the role of women in that society, or the types of food and non alcoholic beverages that would be permissible for Arabian guests on board the plane. Being able to write a sentence or two mentioning your understanding of this will go a long way toward getting that interview, and is the type of information that will definitely gain the interviewer's attention.

Lastly, you should request that after they read your resume they contact you as soon as possible to set up an interview. When they do, make sure you are available. Do not fold your cover letter or resume. Instead they should be placed in a large envelope with a stamped self-addressed envelope. Finally, make sure you have enough postage to cover the cost of mailing both of them.

SAMPLE COVER LETTER

17 Orchard Street
Seattle, WA 59776
(506) 776-XXXX
Suehealy@abc.com

December 12, 2000

Pacific Sporting and Fishing Corporation
Harbor Blvd.,
Seattle, WA 59778

Attn: John Hansen, Crewmember recruitment

Dear Mr. Hansen,

I am currently seeking employment as a corporate flight attendant. You will see by my resume that I have completed all the necessary Part 135 training as well as numerous other courses that I feel would make me as asset to your flight department. These include:

- Fluency in the Japanese language.
- A thorough knowledge of sporting clothes and equipment gained from two years as a part-time sporting goods salesperson.
- Certified in cross-cultural food preparation and service.

Some other highlights include one year as a foreign exchange student in New Zealand and a one-month fishing expedition with Wayfarers' Adventures where I became familiar with deep sea fishing and trawling.

I would like to have the opportunity of meeting with you to discuss my qualifications in greater detail, as well as my eagerness to join your company as a corporate flight attendant. I have enclosed a stamped, self-addressed envelope and would appreciate a reply at your earliest convenience.

Thank you for your consideration and time.

Sincerely,

Susan Healy

encl.2

BUSINESS CARDS

Business cards are actually advertising statements on what you want to say about yourself to other people. What appears on the face of the card is the impression people are going to have about you long after you've gone, so it's vital that you convey the right message to get and keep their attention.

There are two basic things you must put on your card:

- Personal information: Your name, address and contact numbers (cell phone, home telephone, e-mail, beeper).
- Professional information: What your profession and specialization is. (If you are new to the business use the last style.)

It's best to keep the style plain and simple such as a white card with black or gold printing. If you're really creative you may come up with a novel idea, but the printing fees will probably determine the type of style you choose. Buy them in bulk and mail or give them out to everyone in the aviation industry; no one is going to know you exist if you keep them hidden in a box in your drawer.

SAMPLE BUSINESS CARD

Judy Douglas
EXECUTIVE FLIGHT ATTENDANT
(Gulfstream II, III, IV, Challenger)

706-554-XXXX   voice mail
706-765-XXXX   cell phone
Judy @abc.xxx   email

P.O. Box 3204, Orange,
California, 92265

7211 Shady Lane, Orange,
California, 92265

PAUL JOHNSON
CORPORATE FLIGHT ATTENDANT

810-224-XXXX 24 hours/voice mail
810-765-XXXX pager

7 Hislop Street, Palmerston, California, 92712

WHERE TO SEND YOUR RESUME

Perhaps the best place to distribute your resume first is where you go for your flight attendant training. While you are there announce that you are looking for a job and give everyone a resume along with two of your business cards – one to keep and one to pass on to someone else in the business. A number of flight attendants have found jobs through meeting up with other crews going to the same training facility. You may also want to send your resume and business cards to other training companies as well.

Today many aviation companies are connected to the Internet, so if you have access do a search there. This is one profession where personnel tend to look out for each other and are quick to help in any way they can. Usually an e-mail requesting information will generate quicker response than writing a letter. Of course a phone call will also work, but this could add up to some hefty charges if you call long distance. Listed below are some of the main aviation recruitment companies that may assist you in your search.

Bizjetpilot.com; 888-257-9697 or 818-988-5015; website www.bizjetpilot.com
A website that allows flight attendants to list their resume online so that corporations can search for one according to their qualifications, location and availability. There is no charge to the flight attendant.

Jet Professionals, Inc., 800-441-6016, website www.jet-professionals.com
This company hires both qualified temporary and permanent corporate flight attendants.

Corporate Aviators, Inc., 203-426-3032, website www.corporateaviators.com

Another good source is to check the Yellow Pages of your telephone directory to find the airport listings. Many airports have aircraft charter companies who manage aircraft and hire temporary and permanent flight crews to operate them. Call all the companies based at the airport and ask if there are any positions available for a flight attendant within their company. If the response is negative ask them if they could give you a name and phone number of a company who does. Once you connect with a company that hires flight attendants send them your resume to keep on file in case they should have a need for you in the future. Often flight attendants have been hired this way before the position even became public knowledge.

While there are no main corporate flight attendant magazines on the market today there are a number of aviation magazines that may be of use to you because of the worthwhile information contained in their classified sections. Two of them are:

Professional Pilot
TEL: 703-370-0606
www.propilotmag.com

Business & Commercial Aviation
TEL: 914-939-0300
www.AviationNow.com

LOG BOOK

It's important to keep a Log Book listing the date you mailed your resume, the company it was sent to, the telephone number, address, and the name of the contact person. Also add a column for the date they responded to your resume and what their comments were. This will help you to keep your job search organized and it's also handy as a quick reference for tax deductions at the end of the year.

Make sure that you have the correct names of the contact person, company and address. If you do not know the correct spelling of the names then call and ask the telephone operator for help. Never mail out correspondence with any contact names being spelled incorrectly. It is the height of rudeness because it shows that you don't care enough to get it right and that's not the image you want to project.

It's also a good idea to enclose a stamped self-addressed envelope to ensure that you get a response once you mail something out. Many corporations and flight departments are overwhelmed with job applicants and often it's just not possible to respond to them all. If you have still not received a response after thirty days then send a duplicate. Make sure you enter this on your log each time so that you always have correct records.

SAMPLE LOG BOOK

DATE:_____

COMPANY NAME:_____

CONTACT NAME:_____

ADDRESS:_____

DATE MAILED:_____

RECEIVED REPLY:_____

COMMENTS:_____

FOLLOW-UP:_____

_____

_____

_____

CHAPTER 5: THE EMPLOYMENT PROCESS

Success! One of your stamped, self-addressed envelopes has just come back, or you have received a telephone call, with an offer of an interview. Your first big moment in corporate flight attending has arrived and right now you're feeling the rush of adrenaline that leaves your senses reeling! The next step though is crucial as there are probably numerous candidates all vying for the same position. The key points to remember are being energetic, motivated, charismatic and absolutely capable, and all molded together into a top leadership style of professionalism. Does this sound like you? If not, let's do some fine-tuning.

DO YOU LOOK LIKE A FLIGHT ATTENDANT?

Some prospective flight attendants have edged out their competitors by going to the interview looking like a flight attendant. This obviously helped the interviewer see them in that position, especially when it was the first flight attendant position within that company. My advice is to do the same – dress like a flight attendant, especially if you have never worked as one before and the company holding the interview has never had a plane or a flight attendant of their own before, either. For the ladies a simple navy blue suit with a white or cream blouse, navy pumps and little jewelry (remember the previous chapter?), combined with a matching handbag or maybe a briefcase would be ideal.

If you decide to wear something else, follow the guidelines in the previous chapter and wear a tailored jacket over your skirt, dress or trousers. This always looks great! If you decide to carry your resume, place it along with any copies, references and business cards in a folder and be careful not to crease them.

The men should go wearing dark trousers, white shirt, nice jacket, tie, polished shoes and perhaps carrying a briefcase. This will be handy for carrying the extra copies of your resume and any other paperwork that they might have asked you for. Make sure they are in a protective folder. You must be able to present them to the interviewer looking clean, crisp and without any marks or folds. Don't forget your business cards!

ANSWERING THEIR QUESTIONS

If you are a flight attendant starting out then the following list will be of great help. You should expect to be asked many of these questions during your interview and maybe more. Be prepared!

- **TESTING YOUR MOTIVATION**
  (1) Why do you want to be a corporate flight attendant?
  (2) Why do you want to work with this company?
  (3) What do you know about this company?
  (4) Why should we hire you?
  (5) Have you ever traveled before? With whom?
  (6) What are your personal goals for the next ten years?
  (7) What are your educational goals for the next ten years?
  (8) What are your career goals for the next ten years?

MOTIVATIONAL RESPONSES

These questions are designed to see why you really want to be a flight attendant. Is it because of the free travel, meeting and mixing with the rich and famous or the high income? Of course nearly everyone would probably say yes to all of the above, otherwise why would you consider flying?

There are, however, additional factors to consider. Free travel is definitely a plus, especially when it's usually first class, however the job requires an energized, well-coordinated individual. You can't have one without the other. Your education and career goals must be ones that enable you to be an employee of the company for several years at least. Forget your idea of opening a catering business or restaurant within five years at this time because all your goals should be to fly with this company for a long, long time.

- ## TESTING YOUR PUBLIC RELATIONS SKILLS
  (1) Have you ever spoken in public? If so, for how long? To whom?
  (2) Do you get claustrophobic with lots of people in small areas?
  (3) What type of people do you like to be around?
  (4) Describe your personality in five adjectives.
  (5) What don't people like about you the most?
  (6) What do people like about you the most?
  (7) Have you ever worked under extreme pressure? If so, how did you cope?
  (8) Have you ever held a leadership role within your community?

PUBLIC RELATION RESPONSES

These questions are designed to determine the level of communication you've had within your environment. Your passengers may be quite a mix of society from world leaders to rock and roll musicians. Some of them may be difficult to manage, demanding, or uncomfortable to be around and so your response to these questions will help the interviewer determine how poised you are when faced with a multitude of personalities – often in one person! A calm, easygoing, very much in control, professional attitude is required at all times regardless of the situation, and especially when dealing with tired and jet-lagged passengers and crew, including yourself.

- ## TESTING YOUR EMOTIONAL MATURITY
  (1) Can you live away from home for weeks at a time?
  (2) Describe a high point in your life.
  (3) Describe a low point in your life.
  (4) Why did you leave your last job?
  (5) What did you find the most challenging in your last/present job?
  (6) How do you rate your energy level?
  (7) What do you think would be the easiest/most difficult part of the job for you?

EMOTIONAL MATURITY RESPONSES

Flying around the world in a luxury jet with all expenses paid may sound glamorous, but there is a price to pay. Often you will be away from home and your family and friends for considerable lengths of time. Homesickness, or the desire to be home among familiar things is a common occurrence among flight crews, especially when they are working and living in many of the environments the company chooses and they only have each other for company.

Unfortunately, most people have a difficult time comprehending that flight crews could miss home; after all, they feel that you're doing what nearly everyone yearns to do and that is travel the world for free! Finding a balancing point between the two opinions, your love of travel and the yearning to be home, requires a heightened sense of emotional maturity, especially when it's your family that's involved. A cheerful, positive, emotionally mature outlook on life is required to make this job and your personal life a continued success.

- **TESTING YOUR AVAILABILITY**
  (1) Are you free to travel at a moment's notice?
  (2) What arrangements will you make for your dependents when you travel?
  (3) How much notice do you need to give to your present employer?
  (4) Do you have any concerns that may cause a problem with this job?

AVAILABILITY RESPONSES

Most flight attendant jobs become available quickly and are filled just as quickly. Part of the reason for this is that most flight crews network among themselves and so when a position becomes available, most will know about it. You need to ensure that your availability will be soon because if they decide to hire you, they will have to pay for freelance workers until you arrive. Some of you may want to consider temporary work, in an office, for example, so that you will be available immediately.

- **TESTING YOUR WORK HABITS**
  (1) What do/did you like about your present/past job?
  (2) What do/did you like least about your present/past job?
  (3) Can you work independently?
  (4) How many sick days have you had in the last two years?
  (5) Describe your ideal workday.

WORK HABIT RESPONSES

These questions are designed to see if you can handle the irregular, fast-paced workload of a corporate flight attendant. If you're the type of person who watches the clock to see when it's closing time or your sick days outnumber your workdays, then this job is definitely not for you. If your ideal working environment is working alone in a darkroom processing photos, or typing on a computer in a six-by-four cubicle, then this job is definitely not for you. As a corporate flight attendant you will soon realize that the word "routine" does not exist. You will be faced with numerous departure and arrival changes, flight cancellations and additions, irregular hours, catering changes, frustrated passengers, flight crew and so on. You must be able to adjust quickly and capably to any situation with the minimum of fuss and bother. There is no exception.

Be prepared for some or all of these questions to be asked during your interview. Be truthful in your answers, as it's better to be rejected in the beginning than to be fired at a later date. For some of you, answering these questions may be difficult so you may want to seek assistance from someone in a counseling or human resources environment. The way you respond to the questions will have a great impact upon the interviewer's hiring decision. Just because your employment record is below par, it doesn't mean you can't be hired. It just means that you have to be able to prove that you are now the flight attendant they're looking for.

PREPARING FOR THE INTERVIEW

Your first few moments with the interviewer will probably decide the outcome for the rest of the appointment. If you have followed the previous steps of dressing appropriately and reflecting a cheerful, positive image, then you are off to a good start. Fortunately, a lot of corporate flight attendant interviews are conducted with only one or two interviewers, which is unlike the airlines, where you can expect to be interviewed by a large group.

It's important to remember that your body language tells just as much about you as your appearance and speech. If you are tired, nervous, (and you will be), it will show in the way you walk, sit, move or talk. To counteract this there are a few simple rules to follow that can help give you the confidence and assurance that you will need.

THE DAY BEFORE THE INTERVIEW

Get your hair groomed and nails manicured, and gentlemen – this applies to you, too! Sort out the clothes you will be wearing and ensure that they fit, and look clean and pressed. Place extra copies of your resume in a folder along with any references or award information that may be requested. Once again, do not fold your paperwork.

If you are unsure of where the interview will be held then it's advisable for you to visit the location so that this will not cause you to be late. If you're driving remember to check the parking facilities and don't forget to wash the car. How well you take care of your personal possessions is usually a good indication of how well you would take care of a company's possessions– in this case, an airplane.

THE DAY OF YOUR INTERVIEW

Be on time! To ensure that you will be, leave earlier than usual and allow for time to park your car, walk to the building, greet the receptionist and gather your composure. Upon entering do not fidget, jingle the coins in your pocket or talk too loudly. Calmly introduce yourself to the receptionist (if there is one), and take a seat. Listen carefully to what the receptionist is saying and don't agree or disagree with anything that is negative concerning the company environment because that person may very well be the flight attendant you are replacing, or the one who makes the final hiring decision.

DURING THE INTERVIEW

When meeting your interviewer make sure that you are standing straight and presenting a calm and professional manner. Genuinely smile and give a firm handshake to let them know you are really happy to be there. Eye contact is important, so look directly at them when they (and you) are talking. No matter what the distractions are around the room, give them your full attention. Do not hitch or tug at your clothing and refuse all offers of drinks or food to avoid spills or choking. Once seated, sit erect in the chair and place your briefcase or purse on the floor beside you and remember to smile sincerely because seldom does a furrowed brow or wandering eye gain acceptance.

Answer the questions calmly and slowly and if you have done your homework from the previous section, you should be able to answer them quite confidently. Nervousness tends to make a person raise their voice and wave their hands about in excited agitation, so take a deep breath (when no one's watching), and stay calm. In finishing, thank them for their time and ask them when you can expect to hear from them, and on your way out, don't forget to shake their hand firmly again and say good-bye to the receptionist as well.

AFTER THE INTERVIEW

The following day send a thank-you note to the interviewer saying how much you appreciated the opportunity to interview for the position as their flight attendant. Be sincere! If by the appointed time, you have not heard from them, then you should send another note or call their office. Often the interviewer is the Pilot-In-Command, who has not been able to get back to you or anybody else because they are away on a trip. Sometimes there are so many applicants that sorting through them all is difficult. By keeping in touch you not only show your eagerness to be part of their aviation team, but also ensures your name becomes more familiar.

Make sure that you detail all the calls and correspondence made to each company by recording the information in your log book. This will ensure that you have accurate records both for tax purposes as well as updated information on your job hunting prospects. Be prepared for rejection. When this happens you may want to send a note saying that they can still contact you in the future, if the position should once again open up and you are available. There have been many occasions when someone has been hired for a job and a week later quit or was fired. The key point here is to never give up.

GREAT NEWS!

Congratulations – you're hired! These are the words you've been waiting to hear. Fantastic! Now that you finally have a job as a corporate flight attendant, it's time to prepare for another incredible challenge – how to travel the world while living out of a suitcase.

CHAPTER 6: PREPARING TO TRAVEL

Perhaps the best dressed and most organized travelers in the world are flight crewmembers and yet the only luggage they carry are usually two pieces. How do they do it? It's called "coordination" and the following will, I hope, help you to do the same.

BUYING THE RIGHT LUGGAGE

Flight crewmembers usually carry one hard case on wheels with an expandable handle and one fold-up bag they can attach to it. That way there is no heavy lifting of bags and with the ease of mobility in pulling the luggage instead of lifting it, when they move they just look a whole lot better. You are going to do the same.

The hard case must be on wheels, sturdy and waterproof. The expandable handle must be strong enough to support the weight of the soft fold-up bag placed on top of it. A hard case is necessary to protect items that may be damaged on the journey. Into this you would put your toiletries (enclosed in ziplock plastic bags), hairdryer, shoes, radios or whatever else that may be breakable.

Your fold-up bag should have solid corners to protect your clothes hanging on plastic coat hangers inside. Avoid using wire hangers as the ends will tear your clothing. It is preferable to buy a fold-up bag that opens vertically as opposed to horizontally as hotel closets around the world are often small and do not provide enough room for the expandable horizontal varieties. The vertical opening bag can hang on a closet rack and the zippered pockets can double as drawers. This saves a tremendous amount of time packing and unpacking when you are constantly on the move.

The space allocated for luggage on private jets is minimal, especially on the smaller jets, so there will not be room for excess or unusually sized baggage. For this reason you will also appreciate the hard case as many bags will be placed on top of it. Another reason is that when your aircraft arrives at its destination, baggage handlers will often do the loading of the luggage onto a cart and in many places, they are more concerned with getting the job done quickly than worrying about the fragility of a suitcase.

For the ladies it is also a good idea to have a large leather purse with detachable strap in which to carry your personal items. Men could carry a briefcase, backpack or shoulder bag.

HOW AND WHAT TO PACK

The secret to minimum luggage and getting it all to fit into the two cases above is color coordination. This means you use one or two basic colors and highlight them with accessories. Now you know why men don't have the same problem packing as women do because they are limited to a few colors only.

You may want to invest in a clothes rack so that it's easier to see the color-coordinated outfits before they are packed. Of course, what you pack also depends on what part of the world you are going to and the season; however, although the fabric may change (wool to cotton), the color code should stay the same. Also be aware that drycleaning facilities are not always available around the world and even if they were, if your stay is only one night, there wouldn't be time to get it done anyway. When packing keep this is mind.

Assuming that you have already worked out your uniform requirements, use the following as a guide. You will find that all the pieces can be inter-matched for every part of your wardrobe and that they will fit into the two pieces of luggage you are going to be carrying.

WOMEN

BASIC COLOR – BLACK

    1 black dress
    1 black pair of pants
    1 black skirt

    Add to this:
    1 black/brown/gold matching belts
    2 plain washable silk blouses in maybe cream or white
    2 tailored blazer/jackets in maybe beige or green
    scarves/jewelry/accessories
    1 pair of jeans

    Include shoes:
    1 pair black pumps
    1 pair flats/sandals
    1 pair of athletic shoes

    The black dress could be worn to a formal occasion and by adding one of the jackets, it would look great at church, a business meeting, or even a dinner. The same combination goes for the pants. Combine the black pants with a silk shirt, add a jacket, black pumps and perhaps a scarf, and you have a professional looking outfit. Remove the jacket and scarf and you could romp along the beach with your athletic shoes on - or off, whichever you prefer.

    Make up your own color combinations by using this list, being careful to place the same color you choose into each piece; for example, if cream is your basic color choice then wherever you see "black," replace it with cream and so on.

MEN

BASIC COLOR - BLACK. The same combinations work equally well for men.

    1 pair black trousers
    1 pair tan trousers

    Add to this:
    1 each - black and brown leather belts
    2 plain cotton or washable silk shirts, maybe in cream or white
    2 tailored jackets, maybe in light gray and navy blue
    pocket handkerchiefs, tie tacs, ties, accessories
    1 pair of jeans

    Include shoes:
    1 pair black
    1 pair brown
    1 pair athletic shoes

Using this combination you will find that a pair of black trousers go well with a white shirt and gray jacket or the tan pants go well with a cream shirt and navy blue jacket. The jackets and shirts also combine to make a great casual outfit when combined with the jeans. Take off the jacket, add some athletic shoes and you have a great outfit to romp along the beach as well! The point to remember from both of these combinations is that you will always have something casual, professional or formal to wear at any time.

ADDITIONAL ITEMS TO PACK

NIGHT ATTIRE

BATHROBES

These should be lightweight and nonsee-through. Remember, you will be answering hotel doors, speaking to maids in your room, or in rare cases, evacuating the building, so be prepared!

SLEEPWEAR

A pair of sweats works great when traveling to cold weather environments and also doubles as a jogging or lounge suit to relax in. Once again, sleepwear should be lightweight and nonsee-through.

SLIPPERS

If you're really trying to save space in your luggage then socks can be worn instead of slippers. (It's also a good idea to buy a pair of mesh shoes or something similar to wear in the shower to prevent your feet from touching floor surfaces which can, in some places, be contaminated. Unfortunately, hotels around the world are not required to meet the American hotel standards and so it is advisable to be prepared.)

CASUAL ATTIRE

RAINCOAT

When you buy a raincoat try to find one with a detachable inner shell, preferably in a fur or wool type fabric. One of the best to buy is the London Fog coat, which is heavy-duty, waterproof and has a detachable shell inside, along with a detachable hood. The outer shell will protect you from the wind and rain and the inner shell will provide the extra warmth for the cold. Your coat, in many cases, will double as a blanket and a pillow, especially when you travel to some of the impoverished countries where everything, including bedding, is scarce.

JEANS

These are generally an acceptable item of clothing almost anywhere in America; however, in some parts of the world they are not considered as such. It's advisable to still pack some as you will be able to wear them at some point of your journey even if it's in your hotel room. If you take a good quality pair with no holes, ragged edges, or obvious stains and add a tailored jacket, you will probably find that they will be accepted in places where jeans are not the preferred standard of clothing.

SNOW CLOTHES

It is preferable to leave a small bag containing a ski-jacket, mittens/gloves, hat, mask and boots on board the plane for those unexpected moments when you will travel across several weather patterns. An example would be going from Los Angeles to Iceland. In Los Angeles during autumn the temperatures may be a sunny seventy degrees; however, when you stop to refuel at New Foundland the temperature could be minus 30 degrees and snowing. Once the plane lands there you will probably have to leave your cozy environment to check on your catering and supplies in the terminal. Having that ski bag full of accessories onboard will be most appreciated when you step outside.

FOOTWEAR

All shoes, boots and sneakers should be kept in shoe bags and placed in the hard-case bag to prevent damage. It's quite a task in some countries to find shoes that fit if a pair happens to get damaged along the way. Westerners on the average tend to have larger feet than those in the East and so if your shoes get damaged en route, finding a replacement pair in those countries can be difficult. Always carry spares of the main color with you, or if possible, buy two identical pairs and that way you will always be prepared.

MISCELLANEOUS

JEWELRY

You are strongly advised to leave all your expensive pieces of jewelry at home as there really is no safe place to keep them once you start to travel. Some flight crew have a jeweler make duplicates of their treasures and wear these instead; however, anything that looks of value usually stands out and still leaves you a good target for robbers. Least is best.

UNIFORMS

Most of you will be required to wear a uniform and there are many advantages to wearing them. They eliminate the problem of what to wear when working and this requires less packing of regular clothes.

It is advisable to keep a spare uniform on board and change into it upon your arrival or departure if time permits. This helps to reduce the amount of weight and bulk you carry around in your bags at each location.

TOILETRIES

Keep all of your containers containing liquid and creams in enclosed plastic bags. Items such as hairspray, shampoos and conditioners, makeup, lotions, medicines, etc. can explode under pressure at high altitude. The resulting damage to the contents of your luggage when these items are not enclosed in plastic bags, hardly needs to be explained.

Most hotels will provide you with some sort of hand or bath soap; however, in some countries soap, hair products, tissues and often toilet rolls, are considered a luxury and are not supplied. Always make sure you take these with you when you travel.

MEDICINES

It is presumed that you will be in excellent physical health when you leave on your journeys; however, nothing can guarantee that you will stay feeling well or accident free for the duration of the trips. It is advisable for you to carry a spare pair of glasses and any medications, if necessary.

FLASHLIGHTS

Always keep one to use on the plane and one to take with you when you leave.

BATTERIES/ADAPTER KITS

Always keep a good supply of new batteries on you. It's surprising how many you go through with all your travel accessories. They run the flashlights, CD players, ham radios, shavers, alarm clocks, watches and much more. Rechargeable batteries are great but make sure you take along the international converter kit to charge them with. These are essential electrical aids that convert current so that you can use your appliances outside of America. Look for the type that automatically switches to the correct voltage setting from high to low. Also purchase adapter plugs, telephone jack adapters and surge protectors if you plan to use a computer and/or a modem.

STEAM IRON

A travel steamer is great for eliminating wrinkles on everything from heavy-duty fabrics to soft silks. Buy a dual voltage 120/140 voltage, or carry an adapter kit, so that you can use it worldwide.

DUMMY WALLETS

This is one of the best items when traveling and can save you a lot of stress in the event of a theft. While your real wallet lies hidden on your body, your fake wallet, complete with useless cards collected from those sent to you by vendors in the mail, plus some cash, will be what you give out if ever you are robbed. Some clothing manufacturers are now including hidden pockets inside clothing, which are great for hiding that real wallet and all your valuables. Where possible, buy these as well.

PACKING LIST

CLOTHING
Bathrobe (lightweight and nonsee-through
Blouses, shirts, T-shirts
Dresses
Gloves
Jackets
Jeans
Raincoat
Scarves
Shorts
Slippers
Ski jacket – overalls, gloves, socks, hat, and boots
Skirts
Socks, stockings
Suits – jackets, pants, skirts
Sweaters
Swimsuit, cap
Ties
Underwear – pants, bras

CLOTHING ACCESSORIES
Belts
Briefcases
Handbags
Hats
Shoes, sneakers, boots
Umbrella

JEWELRY
Earrings, rings, necklace, pins
Jewelry bag
Spare watch – dual time

TOILETRIES
Bath Soap – small packets
Brush and comb
Contact lens supplies
Cosmetics
Cotton balls, cotton swabs
Dental floss
Deodorant
Feminine supplies
Mouthwash
Nail kits, nail polish, and nail polish remover
Hair bands, hairpins
Hairspray
Razors
Shampoo and conditioner

Shaving cream, aftershave lotion
Shower cap
Suntan lotion, sunburn cream
Tissues
Toothbrush and case, toothpaste
Vitamins, energy bars and snacks

MEDICINES
Allergy medications
Anti-itch cream
Antibiotic cream
Anti-diarrhea tablets
Anti-fungal cream
Bandages, Band-Aids (waterproof)
Cold and flu tablets
Cough medicine
Decongestant
Eardrops
Eyedrops – Visine
Foot cream
Insect repellent
Laxatives
Pain relievers, headache tablets
Scissors, tweezers
Thermometer

MISCELLANEOUS
Batteries
Books, magazines
Bottled water
Boot/shoe polish
Camera, flash, batteries
Cellular telephone, charger, batteries
Clothes brush
Coffee pot – (traveler's), coffee, sugar, creamer
Computer, batteries, cords, paper, copier, ink
Dummy wallet with cash
Ham radio, antennas, and batteries
International power adapters
Maps
Passport, visas, greencard
Radio cassette player, tapes, CD player, discs, batteries
Sewing kit, scissors
Stationery – envelopes, paper, stamps
Sunglasses
Travel alarm clock
Travel iron
Waterproof gel/spray for boots, shoes and coat

HOUSEHOLD ARRANGEMENTS

POST OFFICE BOX
If you live alone you may want to consider investing in a post office box so that your mail will not pile up at home leaving your away status obvious. If you make prior arrangements with the post office they will usually hold your mail for an indefinite time until you return.

NEWSPAPER
As a security factor it is best to cancel the delivery if there is no one at home to collect it every day.

BILLS
If you don't have an automatic payment system with your bank you may want to prepay or overpay your bills so that you won't be caught with late charges or disconnected utilities when you return home.

AUTOMATIC LIGHTING
A good way to deter burglars while you're traveling is to install automatic light switches throughout your residence and keep a radio going so that it gives the appearance that someone is at home.

OUTDOOR GARDEN AND ENVIRONMENT
Pool and spa equipment must be maintained on a regular weekly basis and if it's neglected, is very expensive to repair or replace. The garden sprinklers need to be adjusted according to the season you live in as well. A month's absence can do a lot of damage to your outdoor area if proper care is not maintained and so you are advised to seek the help of someone to do this for you.

PERSONAL ARRANGEMENTS

MEDICAL CHECKUP
It's highly recommended that you have a complete physical, including optical and dental, before you start on your first job and that you have regular checkups each year following. Although the airlines insist upon a physical before you are hired, in corporate aviation this is often not so, although a drug test may be required.

CORRESPONDENCE
Always carry an address book of some sort that lists all your contact numbers back home. You may not plan to call once you travel, but often journeys are delayed for long periods of time and it becomes necessary to reach the utility companies and others before they turn everything off or adversely affect your credit rating.

You should also leave a copy of your trip sheet with a family member or friend containing all the information of where you can be reached in the event of an emergency.

AIRLINE/HOTEL/RENTAL CAR INFORMATION

You should secure an updated listing of all the hotels, airlines and car rental agencies as you will be referring to this list frequently. They are readily available on the Internet, or via the Yellow Pages telephone directory. There may be an occasion when your company will ask you to take a public airline flight home rather than stay away on the trip. At the end of the appointed time you will then have to fly back to bring the passengers home in your plane. Quick access to this information will make it a lot easier, especially when you are overseas.

One of the benefits of working as a corporate flight attendant is that you accrue a lot of points on the airline, hotel and rental car membership programs. These points can eventually be traded in for free trips and merchandise and a host of other benefits, so they are a very welcome bonus to your job. To become a member you simply sign up at the check-in counters wherever you go and periodically you will receive a statement advising you of your total points and what you can receive for them.

Many of these companies offer bonus incentives for you to use their membership programs such as concierge services and upgraded accommodation according to the level you have reached. Points can also be accumulated by using one of their credit cards and often these cards receive double or triple points if you use it in their facility, such as a hotel gift shop. It's a great way to get a few treats while you're working so sign up for them whenever you can. Of course, if you use a company credit card they will get the benefits, not you.

CREDIT CARDS

A major credit card is essential when you become a flight attendant. Some companies will give you a company credit card, but most will expect you to have one of your own. You will need one to secure accommodations, rent a car, buy meals, in fact, almost everything when you are away. At the end of the trip you simply submit an expense report and wait to be reimbursed upon approval of your report.

The advantage to having your own card is that you get to keep the points offered in those membership programs and you can build up your credit considerably. If you have had credit problems in the past and have difficulty securing another credit card, then apply for a secured debit card. These cards are attached to a savings account and can be used up to the amount of money you have invested in the savings plan. In this plan you decide how much cash you want to deposit and a card will be issued against that amount. You will probably need to deposit at least $2,000-$3,000 because hotel accommodation costs can mount up quickly, especially when overseas.

The most widely accepted cards worldwide are the American Express, Visa and MasterCard.

PART TWO: BEFORE THE FLIGHT

CHAPTER 7: ORGANIZING THE PAPERWORK

An important part of your preparation work involves organizing various lists and keeping them updated so that each of your trips will run smoothly. You cannot rely on memory as fatigue and jet lag will eventually catch up with you and mistakes will happen. I'm sure every flight attendant has at least one story they can tell you where something significant was forgotten or left behind. The lucky ones got to keep their jobs.

In this section the following topics will be covered:

- Passenger Profile Lists
- Aircraft Supplies List
- Caterer's List
- Departure and Arrival Checklist
- Welcome Aboard Booklets
- Briefing Cards

PASSENGER PROFILE LISTS

Where possible, ask your passengers to complete one of these lists prior to their arrival on board. If this is not possible, ask someone to obtain this information for you. Upon receipt of the lists, place them into a Passenger Profile Log in alphabetical order. When a trip is planned you will then go through them and select the appropriate one for each of the passengers and then you can plan your catering and any special needs accordingly.

Religious and cultural customs, plus personal preferences, can determine what a passenger will eat, drink or participate in. Orthodox Jews, for example, don't eat pork, while Muslims forbid alcohol. In planning your catering you must ensure that these special needs are met, unless of course you are advised by the passengers themselves, or your boss, to do otherwise.

Pay special attention to the following three areas:

- **DISLIKES:**

Obviously, if they have written something here you should do everything possible to meet their needs. Perhaps it's the smell of a food item such as garlic or seafood so where possible, minimize this or eliminate it completely. Perhaps they suffer from hot flashes which makes any temperature above sixty degrees a heat wave! Without sacrificing the comfort of others, you would lower the cabin temperature slightly and then ensure their seating area is cooled down with the overhead air vent before they arrive. Once they arrive, you would make them comfortable with either a cool drink, a personal ice pack or perhaps a spray mister, even if it's only fifty degrees Fahrenheit!

A comfortable passenger is usually a happy passenger and this will ensure future flights will be a continued success. Once they are on board it's your duty to find out, as much as possible, what their needs are so that you can personalize their service and make it better for them the next time. Jot down any extra notes you observe during each flight you have with them. By doing this, you will find that after several flights you will be able to care for them before they even have to ask, and that's what will help to set you apart as a superior flight attendant.

- **ALLERGIES:**

Top priority should be given to replace or remove anything that could induce an allergic reaction such as flowers, certain foods, or even cleaning chemicals in the carpet. A private jet, such as a Gulfstream, usually flies at an altitude above forty thousand feet and in the event of an emergency, you must take into consideration that it will take approximately twenty minutes to descend and land. Add to this the additional time a control tower must take to divert other air traffic so your plane can fly safely through that airspace, and you have a considerable time lapse before help can arrive. Unfortunately, this time lapse may be too long for your ailing passenger, so prevention in the beginning is far better than any unwanted emergency.

- **OTHER:**

     Perhaps the most common note here is "fearful flyer." If so, try to contact the passenger before the flight and attempt to dispel any fears they may have of flying. Where possible, coordinate a tour with the aviation manager or chief pilot and invite them for a tour of the plane days before their trip to familiarize them with everything from the cockpit to the baggage compartment. Often, having one of the pilots explain to them how the plane flies is enough to reduce their fears considerably. Flying in a private jet has its advantages because it's easier to distract them with the luxurious ambiance and personal attention they will receive from you.

     Perhaps they travel frequently with their pet. This is quite common and so you should make provisions for the animal as well as checking on other passengers to make sure no one suffers from allergies. If so, both parties - the pet owner and the allergic passenger, - should be informed and then work with their needs accordingly. Remember, their success is your success.

PASSENGER PROFILE LIST

COMPANY: _____ CONTACT # _____

NAME:_____ BIRTHDATE: _____

TITLE:_____ ANNIVERSARY:_____

BREAKFAST:_____

_____

LUNCH:_____

DINNER:_____

SNACKS:_____

BEVERAGES:_____

MISCELLANEOUS

NEWSPAPERS/MAGAZINES:_____

RELIGION: _____

MEDICINES/PERSONAL ITEMS:_____

MUSIC/MOVIES:_____

ENTERTAINMENT (GAMES/CARDS):_____

FLOWERS:_____

DISLIKES:_____

ALLERGIES: _____

OTHER:_____

AIRCRAFT SUPPLIES LIST

The following aircraft supplies list is extensive and probably has many items you feel you may never need to use. In a lot of flight departments this is absolutely true; however, there are a few that do. In the event you are hired by one of the few, then the following information will greatly assist you.

In America it is common to get good quality catering at most locations; however, in some places overseas you will have to provide everything yourself because often your plane is the best "restaurant" in town. It's what flight attendants call "camping out jet style." Many a flight attendant has had to cater to on-board meetings and meals in various parts of the world using only the supplies they brought with them. The responsibility is awesome when you consider that some of these "ramp" meetings may amount to millions of dollars in business transactions for your company and how you cater to those on board can often make or break the deal, along with your job.

The following list covers most of the items you will need to buy, stock or replenish on a regular basis. It is extensive so you may want to customize it for your type of flying. Sometimes it helps to list passenger names beside items as a memory aid. Highlight those that are required on each flight as this makes it easier to scan to ensure nothing is forgotten. Items such as newspapers, magazines, milk, juice, bottled water, coffee and ice, fit into this category. After a few trips you will have these memorized, but once again you are strongly advised against doing anything from memory in the beginning, especially when the pace is hectic and you're jet lagged. Always use a check list.

Space is limited in a galley so only take the amount needed for each segment of the trip, plus a few spares. An important note here is that refrigeration is only available when the aircraft engines are running or the auxiliary power is turned on. Often the only refrigeration you will have will be a drawer or small cupboard filled with ice, so great care must be taken with the amount of food, and the type of food, that requires cold storage. Meat, poultry and seafood, for example, should be stored at 38 - 40 degrees and so the more food you pack into these cold storage areas, the longer it takes to keep them at the right temperature.

A good flight attendant is extremely efficient in managing space and they seem to have an innate talent for condensing everything to a minimum and using every inch possibly available. They do this by using containers that are of similar shapes and sizes that can be packed and stored with minimum waste of area. Round and odd angled containers take up a lot of space and are difficult to stack and place in order. Because of this, you are advised to purchase supplies that also come in easy to stack containers. This applies to all areas of the cabin including the galley and bathroom areas. If the supplies you need come in odd sizes then you may want to transfer the items into yours once on board. Of course, these should be of see-through plastic and clearly labeled to identify what's inside. Perhaps the most important feature of all when purchasing containers is to make sure that they are unbreakable, microwaveable and dishwasher safe.

AIRCRAFT SUPPLIES LIST

GALLEY

CUPBOARD
Air freshener
Aluminum foil – gold, silver
Baby foods, disposable bottles, diapers, wipes, lotions
Biscuits – sweet, savory
Candies – chocolates, jellybeans, licorice
Capers
Cards – birthday, anniversary, thank-you, holiday
Corn – canned
Chewing gum
Coffee – regular, decaffeinated
Creamers – packets
Dog/cat food, treats, bowls
Doilies – white, silver, gold, all sizes
Dried fruits – raisins, apricots, dates
Fish – canned, tuna, sardines, anchovies, salmon
Garlic powder
Hearts of palm - canned
Instant soups –packet, canned, jars
Juice – packaged, canned
Lemon juice
Nuts – mixed, salted, unsalted
Oil – salad, cooking, dipping
Packets – instant rice, beans, soups
Pasta – spaghetti, angel hair, ravioli
Pastes
Pate – chicken, duck, goose, liver, port wine
Prunes – whole, pitted
Pretzels, popcorn
Salt, regular, iodized, sea-salt
Seafood-canned, oysters, mussels, anchovies
Sugar – white, brown, cubed, confectioner's,
Sweeteners
Tacos, tostados – soft, hard
Tea – tea bags
Vinegar

REFRIGERATOR
Bagels
Birthday cake, candles, decorations
Bread – white, brown, wheat, rye, sourdough
Breakfast rolls – muffins, Danish, donuts
Buns – dinner rolls, hamburger, hot-dog
Cake
Caviar – Beluga

Cheese – cheddar, Parmesan, Swiss,
Cream cheese – low-fat, regular, flavored
Dips – crackers
Dressings – salad
Dry ice
Eggs
Frozen yogurt, sherbet
Ice cream, cones
Margarine, butter
Mayonnaise
Milk – regular, non-fat
Olives – (fresh) green, black, stuffed, pitted
Peanut Butter
Pickles – dill, Kosher, sweet
Pizza sauce, toppings
Potato salad, macaroni salad, coleslaw
Quiche
Salsa – hot, medium, mild
Sauces – sweet, savory, Horseradish
Sushi – wasabi, ginger, soy sauce
Waffles

MEAT, SEAFOOD AND POULTRY
Bacon
Beef
Chicken
Corned beef
Deli – beef, turkey, ham, pastrami
Ham
Lamb
Pork
Seafood – prawns, cracked crab claws, oysters, mussels
Seafood – salmon, halibut, trout, lobster
Steak – T-bone, porterhouse, New York, sirloin
Turkey
Veal

FRUITS AND VEGETABLES
Alfalfa sprouts
Apples
Apricots
Artichokes
Asparagus
Avocados
Bananas
Berries – blueberries, strawberries, raspberries, blackberries
Broccoli
Cabbage
Carrots
Cauliflower

Celery
Cilantro
Cucumbers
Dill
Edible flowers
Garlic
Grapes – seedless, red, white
Guavas
Kiwis
Lemons
Lettuce – romaine, iceberg
Limes
Mangoes
Melons
Mushrooms
Oranges
Papayas
Parsley
Pears
Pineapple
Plums
Potatoes
Radishes
Red cabbage
Rosemary
Shallots, spring onions
Snow peas
Tomatoes – cherry, regular

HERBS AND SPICES
Basil
Bay Leaves
Chilies
Cinnamon
Cumin
Ground cloves
Lemon pepper
Nutmeg
Onion flakes
Oregano
Paprika
Pepper – black, red, cayenne, ground
Rosemary
Thyme

BAR SUPPLIES
Bacardi
Bar napkins
Beer – lager, ale
Bitters

Bottle - opener, corkscrew, can opener
Brandy
Champagne- sweet, dry
Cognac
Cointreau
Gin
Ice, ice scoop
Ice bucket
Ice chest
Lemons, limes
Liquor miniatures
Maraschino cherries
Olives/onions
Orange juice, grapefruit juice, tomato juice
Perrier water, Pellegrino
Port wine
Rum
Scotch
Sodas – Coca-Cola, 7-Up, club soda, tonic
Water, ginger ale, lemonade
Tequila and mix
Towels
Trays with glass holders
Vermouth – sweet, dry
Vodka
Water pitcher
Whiskey
Wine –red, white, sweet, dry, sparkling, splits

GALLEY EQUIPMENT
Ashtrays
Blender
Bowls
Bread baskets
Brushes – pastry, oil/butter glazer
Butter curler, butter dishes
Canape cutters
Coffee grinder
Coffee pot, extra pots, thermos
Cookware –(nonstick) saucepans and lids, casserole dishes, skillet,
Cutting boards, chopping block
Dinner service (enough for 24 people)
Food/drink funnels
Forks – bayonet, carving
Garlic press
Garnishing tools
Glasses
Grater, shredder
Ice chests – 3-4
Jugs –water, juice, milk

Juice extractor
Knives – paring, fillet, bread, serrated, steak, carving,
Matches
Measuring spoons/cups
Microwave bowls, and lids – all sizes
Microwave, convection oven
Mini mincer, chopper
Napkins – paper, material, all sizes
Napkin rings – plain, decorative
Oven mitts, apron
Paper plates, cups, bowls
Paper towels
Pitchers – water, gravy, creamers
Platters, display plates
Ramkins, sauce dishes
Salt and pepper shakers, condiment containers
Serving spoons
Shears
Silverware (enough for 24 people)
Slicer
Spatula
Strainers, colander, sieve
Thermometer
Tongs
Toothpicks with frill tops
Trash bags
Trays – serving food, passenger lap trays
Vacuum cleaner
Whip, whisks, food mixer

BATHROOM/LAVATORY/CLEANING SUPPLIES

Antacids
Bandaids
Carpet cleaner
Chemical – lavatory
Clorox
Coat hangers – plastic, wooden, cedar
Dental floss
Deodorant – male, female
Deodorizers – antiseptic
Detergent
Dish-mop, sponges
Disinfectant
Disposable gloves
Earplugs
Eyedrops – contact lens solution
Facecloths
Feminine napkins, tampons
First-aid kit/ thermometer

Glass cleaner
Hairbrush, comb, mirror
Hand creams, moisturizers, spray misters
Headache medicines, flu remedies
Insect repellent
Lozenges – sore throat, cough
Mouthwash
Nail polish, remover, files
Nasal spray
Paper cups
Plastic bags – ziplock
Plastic cutlery
Polish – shoe
Polish – silver, brass, gold
Razor blades, shaving cream, aftershave
Sewing repair kit
Shampoo, conditioner, hairspray
Shoe repair kit
Soap – travel size, pump
Tissues
Toilet rolls – regular, aircraft
Toothbrush, toothpaste
Toothpicks
Trash Bags
Travel sick pills
Wet towel wipes

CABIN SUPPLIES

Air sick bags
Atlas - USA, world
Batteries
Bedding – blankets, sheets, pillows, pillow cases, mattresses – regular and inflatable
Cameras – disposable with flashlight, photo album
Cards – playing
Flowers
Lap blankets
Life rafts
Life vests (1 for each seat)
Magazines
Music CDs, videos, TV/board games, cards
Newspapers
Passenger briefing cards
Pencils, pens, sharpeners, stationery, stamps
Seatbelt extenders

COCKPIT SUPPLIES

Antacids
Flashlights and batteries
Notepads/pens
Tissues
Trash bags
Water – bottled

BAGGAGE COMPARTMENT

Luggage ties
Food storage chests

HANGAR

Cart – large 2 tier on wheels
Dishwasher
Icemaker
Large trash cans
Refrigeration
Stepladder
Storage cupboards – food, cleaners, linen, crockery and utensils
Washing machine and dryer

GIFTS

Books
Boxed chocolates (Godiva), candies, truffles
CDs, videos
Company souvenirs
Cups/mugs – designer type
Flowers, corsages
Pen and pencil sets, stationery sets
Perfumes, colognes, aftershave
Souvenirs/artifacts

LIST OF CATERERS

You will also need to establish and keep current a list containing information on the best caterers available worldwide or those you expect to visit. You can obtain these by contacting them and requesting that they send information to you for your reference. Some air terminals have their own resident caterers, but check first to ensure that the quality of service they provide is in keeping with your requirements. You are not obligated to purchase from them just because you are using their air terminal. Finding a quality caterer and especially one who will be able to prepare the food the way you want, can go a long way in helping to make your journey a much easier and more pleasant one.

Ask the caterer to send you a copy of their in-flight menu and keep these in your Catering File to be used when a trip to that location is planned. Make sure you have the contact name of the person you will be ordering from. It is probably easier to file them alphabetically by country, city and town.

Restaurants, hotels and food service delicatessens are also good sources for catering. The first two, along with airline caterers, will be your best sources when traveling overseas, particularly in third-world countries where sanitation and cleanliness are a problem. A general rule with flight crew is never to buy any catering from food vendors on the street, no matter how great it all may look. Many of the products and produce have been prepared and packaged in unhygienic situations such as contaminated water, and serious illnesses and diseases can result if you fail to obey the rules. This will be covered more extensively in the chapter on international flying.

An important point to remember with caterers also is their times of operation. They may only work from 9A.M. - 5P.M. weekdays, and stay closed on the weekends, so you need to make sure they will be able to prepare and deliver the goods at the time of your flight.

Copies of the lists should be carried with you on each trip so that you can update or refer to them whether you are on board or in your hotel room. Not only does this make it a lot easier in planning the next catered event, but helps to ensure that a mistake is less likely to happen.

Always establish a payment method with the caterers before a trip. The usual form of payment is by credit cards or direct billing to the company.

SAMPLE LIST OF CATERERS

ARKANSAS, USA:

XYZ CATERING
Airport Road
Carrollton, AK 71234

PHONE: Business 450-824-XXXX; Cell 450-865-XXXX
CONTACT: Jim Stuart (co-owner/head chef); **Patty** (co-owner, wife, assists).
HOURS OF OPERATION: Open 7 days, 8.00am – 8.00pm. For after hours service call for special arrangements. Extra fee will apply.
DELIVERY: Will deliver to your location. Surcharge if more than 25 miles.
COST: $$$ - Moderate
QUALITY: Superb! Nice presentation, can serve food as is on to tables.
PAYMENT: All major credit cards or will bill company 30 days
REFERRAL: Paulette Nixon (F/A for Jones Flights Srvc.)
NOTES:

****

CALIFORNIA, USA:

ANDY'S KITCHEN
12134 Ventura Lane
Hilton, CA 92261

PHONE: 350-452-XXXX 24 hours/voicemail; FAX: 350-452-XXXX; EMAIL: andy@jplk.xxx
CONTACT: Andy Romano (owner); **Gerald, Lis, Judy and Pepe**
HOURS OF OPERATION: Mon - Fri 7.00 am – 11.00pm. Closed weekends.
DELIVERY: To all airports in district. Please pay driver tip upon delivery.
COST: $$ -Low to moderate
QUALITY: Family style Italian cuisine; tasty! Large portions. One order enough for 2 people.
PAYMENT: Major credit card/cash at time of order. Accounts by prior arrangement only.
REFERRAL: Airport personnel, flight crews
NOTES: Request microwaveable containers necessary. Ask for extra portions of garnishments such as cheese and sauces.

CREATIVE CATERING CONCEPTS
1212 Tulip Lane
Van Nuys, CA 98765

PHONE: 318-567-XXXX 24 hours; FAX: 318-567-XXXX; EMAIL; ccc@ xxx.com
CONTACT: Jennifer or Russ
HOURS OF OPERATION: 24 hours, leave message, response time 10 minutes
DELIVERY: No charge. Beyond 30 miles $15 delivery fee
COST: $$
QUALITY: Excellent food but poor presentation
PAYMENT: All major credit cards, cash, account
REFERRAL: Phone-book at airport counter
NOTES: Ask for the sauces in separate containers. Do decorating yourself. Great for short notice trips. Very reliable!

WEIGHT EQUIVALENTS AND METRIC CONVERSION

You will need to keep this handy when you are ordering in countries outside of the United States otherwise you may end up breaking the budget and having lots of leftovers, if you fail to remember that a kilogram is approximately twice the weight of a pound.

WEIGHT EQUIVALENT

1 kilogram	=	1000 grams
1 ounce	=	28.35 grams
1 pound	=	453.59 grams
1 gram	=	0.03 ounces
100 grams	=	3.53 ounces
1 kilogram	=	35.27 ounces
1 kilogram	=	**2.2046 pounds**

VOLUME EQUIVALENTS

1 liter	=	1000 milliliters
1 teaspoon	=	4.93 milliliters
1 tablespoon	=	14.79 milliliters
1 fluid ounce	=	29.57 milliliters
1 cup	=	237 milliliters
1 pint	=	**473 milliliters**
1 quart	=	946 milliliters
1 gallon	=	**3.78 liters**
1 liter	=	**1.06 quarts**
10 liters	=	**2.64 gallons**

TEMPERATURE EQUIVALENTS

The United States uses the Fahrenheit (F) temperature scale; however, many countries use the metric scale of Celsius (C). This is the easiest way to convert Celsius to Fahrenheit.

1. Multiply the Celsius © number by 9
2. Divide by 5
3. Add 32

DEPARTURE AND ARRIVAL CHECKLISTS

Another checklist you may wish to use in the beginning is the arrival and departure checklist. This will ensure that you have completed everything necessary for the journey ahead and that upon your return, everything is accounted for and ready to be attended to.

SAMPLE DEPARTURE/ARRIVAL CHECKLIST

BEFORE DEPARTURE:

1. Trip sheet received – note departure date and time, # of passengers, catering requested
2. Catering organized
3. Hotel/transportation arranged
4. Passports and visas – crew/passengers
5. Prepare cabin – linens, blankets, bedding, flowers, amusements
6. Check emergency equipment – life vests, life rafts, oxygen, air, fire extinguishers, emergency exits
7. Stock galley – food, beverages, snacks, supplies
8. Dishes, glasses and silverware ready
9. Ice – refrigeration, drinks
10. Newspapers, magazines
11. Weather printouts
12. Bathroom – check water supply, cabinet supplies, medicines
13. Lavatory serviced and working – push button!
14. Water tanks filled
15. Cabin clean – vacuumed, polished, dusted; trash bags emptied
16. "Squawks" list completed
17. Gifts

UPON ARRIVAL:

1. Inventory lists ready
2. Linens ready for laundry/drycleaners
3. Dishes/silverware to be cleaned
4. Lavatory to be serviced by ground personnel
5. Water tanks to be filled
6. Trash ready to be emptied
7. "Squawks" list to Pilot-In-Command
8. Cabin ready for final cleaning

WELCOME ABOARD BOOKLETS

Welcome aboard booklets are always a nice addition to any aircraft although they are not required. Many companies (and it's often the flight attendant) design their own booklets and include information on the plane, the company and the flight crew. A description of the menu, or menus, is often included along with beverages available and any in-flight entertainment, and perhaps details of the intended journey. If these booklets are individualized for special trips then your passengers may want to keep theirs as a memento of their journey. Rejoice! This is always a good indication of how well you did as their flight attendant.

BRIEFING CARDS

Federal aviation regulations Part 91.519 says that the Pilot-In-Command must ensure that all passengers are briefed on:

- Ditching procedures
- Use of flotation devices
- Location of exit and entry doors
- Location and operation of survival equipment
- Operation of emergency exits
- Oxygen – normal and emergency use
- Seat belts and shoulder harnesses
- Smoking

Usually the flight attendant is delegated by the Pilot-In-Command to be the one to give instruction and this may be done either individually or with everyone together. It is further recommended that your aircraft has **Passenger Briefing Cards** as they are a valuable backup to the oral instruction given. These cards must contain information that is applicable to the type and model of aircraft that is being used and to ensure maximum benefit, they should be available for passengers to read at all times.

It is preferable to have pictorial instructions as well as words in the event that some of the passengers do not understand the language it is written in. A three-fold laminated copy will easily fit in a seat pocket and is thus easily seen. Also make sure that the style you choose is laminated and waterproof so that they will last a long time and retain their newness. You may also want to have wallet-sized versions available for the frequent flyers to carry with them.

CHAPTER 8: MEAL PLANNING AND CATERING

Planning meals and organizing the catering is one of the most challenging tasks for corporate flight attendants. They must be able to present a quality, appetizing meal any time of the day or night, in any part of the world, often with limited supplies while working in cramped quarters within a moving aircraft. It takes quite a bit of skill and practice to do all this and end up graciously serving a feast looking fit for a king! If it sounds phenomenal it is; however, this chapter will guide you through all the steps necessary to help make this happen with a minimum of difficulty.

Once a trip is planned and you receive a trip sheet detailing the entire journey, you will need to observe the following:

- **THE DATES AND TIMES OF DEPARTURE AND ARRIVAL**
  Be prepared for the dates and times to continually change, often at a moment's notice. Until the plane is actually departing the runway nothing is certain, and even then the trip can be canceled. Often a trip is delayed a few hours and then the lunch becomes a dinner, or the dinner becomes a midnight snack. You must always be prepared for any last-minute changes and be flexible.

- **NUMBER AND LENGTHS OF LEGS**
  This is crucial in planning your meals. How many legs on the journey? How long between each leg? The time of each leg will thus determine what meal to plan for, and what to prepare.

- **NUMBER OF PASSENGERS ON EACH LEG**
  This will determine the amount of catering required.

- **TYPE OF PASSENGERS**
  Are they Orthodox Jews requiring kosher food or are they strictly vegetarians? Are they diabetic and require sugar-free meals, or are they sumo wrestlers needing larger portions?

- **AGE RANGE OF PASSENGERS**
  Are they adults, teens, children or babies?

- **SPECIAL OCCASION?**
  Is the trip for business, an anniversary, birthday or vacation? Will you need to decorate the plane as well as order special food and supplies?

- **HAS CATERING BEEN ARRANGED FOR THE ENTIRE JOURNEY?**
  If so, you will only need to stock up on accessories such as milk, newspapers, coffee, etc. If not, then you will be required to organize it all.

- **ARE THERE CATERERS AVAILABLE AT EACH LEG OF THE JOURNEY?**
  This will tell you how many supplies you will need on board. If it is within the USA there are many places to buy good quality food from; however, in some of the foreign destinations you may have to take everything with you.

- **ANIMALS?**
  Don't forget the treats!

SAMPLE TRIP ITINERARY

JOHNSON CORPORATION – TRIP SHEET REPORT

TRIP NO: 1234   DESCRIPTION: BUR-TEB-BUR
TRIP DATE: 08/01/00 – 08/03/00
PURPOSE: Business   REQUESTOR: Charles Simonson
TAIL NUMBER: N 777XX   CONTACT PHONE: 346-XXXX

LEG 1	PAX	ZULU +/-		LOCAL	ZULU
KBUR - Burbank	3	-7.0	Tue	08/01 0700	08/01 1400
KTEB – Teterboro		-4.0	Tue	08/01 1500	08/01 1900
ETE: 5.0					

TO: TERMINAL: Millionaire   204-888-XXXX   FAX: 204-889-XXXX
CREW HOTEL: Ritz, Saddlebrook   204-843-XXXX
CREW TRANSPORT: Sedan with driver

LEG INFORMATION

CREW NOTES:
PIC - James Barber, SIC-Carl Higgins; F/A–Vanessa Haines
PASSENGER NOTES:
3 Pax only: Julie Johnson, Marilyn Arnold, Paul Zeiger Snr.
     NOTE: Paul Zieger Snr. – drinks Falls water only – no coffee/alcohol etc.
CATERING:
Pax requested Breakfast: Fruit platter; assorted bagels w/lox & cream cheese; coffee
Pax requested Lunch: Gourmet Mediterranean lunchbox & Perrier/Falls water

---

LEG 2	PAX	ZULU +/-		LOCAL	ZULU
KTEB - Teterboro	5	-4.0	Thu	08/03 1.00PM	08/03 1300
KBOS – Boston		-4.0	Thu	08/03 1.42PM	08/03 1342
ETE: 0.42					

CREW NOTES:
Same.
PASSENGER NOTES:
5 Pax only : Julie Johnson, Marilyn Arnold, Paul Zieger Snr., Jeff Graham, Duane Mellows
CATERING: None required

LEG 3	PAX	ZULU +/-		LOCAL	ZULU
KBOS – Boston	5	-4.0	Thu	08/03 5.00PM	08/03 2100
KBUR – Burbank		-7.0	Thu	08/03 8.00PM	08/03 0300
ETE: 6.0					

CREW NOTES:
Same.
PASSENGER NOTES:
Same as Leg 2.
CATERING: F/A to cater

TERMINAL: Airways Charter Group   301-777-XXXX   FAX:301-777-XXXX

HOW TO INTERPRET A TRIP SHEET FOR CATERING

When you look at the trip sheet on the previous page you will notice that you are **departing on the first of August at seven o'clock in the morning**, Pacific Standard Time. This means that the passengers will be requiring breakfast. If you look in the leg information section of leg 1, you will find that they have requested a breakfast consisting of a fruit platter, assorted bagels with lox and cream cheese, plus beverages. They have not a specified a particular caterer so it will be up to you to either order this from your choice of a caterer, or purchase the items and put it all together yourself. Flight attendants who can do their own catering can save their company thousands of dollars a year in charges, as catered food for an aircraft is unbelievably expensive. Of course, the flight attendant should be able to make it look just as appetizing.

Next you would take into account the number of people who will be eating breakfast. There are three crew members plus three passengers, which totals six. You must also add an additional meal for a last-minute passenger or those wanting second portions, and so now there is a total of **seven breakfasts**.

From this information you would then select the best caterer for that type of food from your list of caterers. Your breakfast order will look like the following:

NOTE: Check with the rest of the crew to see if they will eat what the passengers have ordered, otherwise make additional arrangements for them.

CATERER: Creative Catering Concepts
TEL: 318-567-8XXX
CONTACT: Russ

 # OF BREAKFASTS: 7

1 Fruit Platter consisting of assorted fruits and berries with dipping sauces in separate containers.
2 Assorted bagels (plain, sesame, garlic & onion, blueberry, cheese)
3 Harrod's Lox
4 Cream cheese – regular and low-fat
5 Croissants with assorted jams
6 Orange and grapefruit juice
7 Falls water/coffee

When placing this order with the caterer, seek his advice on the amount of food you will need for seven people. The amounts can differ according to ages (adult, teen or child), and according to the size of the packaging. The meal above will probably cost several hundred dollars and so it's necessary to try to eliminate waste of both food and money where possible.

The second half of leg 1 is the gourmet Mediterranean lunch-box. The estimated time en route to begin with was **five hours (5.0),** however, some of that time has been used in serving breakfast. This means you should allow approximately one hour for breakfast, and after a two hour break, serve their lunch. Again, the total number of lunches to order will also be **seven**.

You may also add any additional items at this stage keeping in mind the prices for newspapers and magazines, for example, will be considerably higher to cover their costs of purchase and delivery. In the end your final catering order will look something like this:

LEG 1

CATERER: Creative Catering Concepts
TEL: 318-567-8989
CONTACT: Russ

OF BREAKFASTS: 7

1   Fruit Platter consisting of assorted fruits and berries with dipping sauces in separate containers.
2   Assorted bagels (plain, sesame, garlic & onion, blueberry, cheese)
3   Harrod's Lox
4   Cream cheese – regular and low-fat
5   Croissants with assorted jams
6   Orange and grapefruit juice
7   Falls water

OF LUNCHES: 7

MEDITERRANEAN LUNCH-BOX

1   Tabouli
2   Falafel
3   Potato Salad
4   Hummus Sauce
5   Baba Ghannouge (eggplant dip)
6   Pita pockets
7   Melon balls/grape cluster

ADDITIONAL:

2 each - Wall Street Journal, USA Today, Burbank Herald newspapers
6 packets - white cocktail napkins
1 pint each – regular milk; low-fat; International vanilla cream
2 dozen Perrier medium
2 dozen Falls - medium
Bunch parsley

DELIVERY:

Russ will deliver 6.00 A.M. to plane.

**Check with guard for Russ to enter airport ramp early a.m.

Leg 2 states that you will be flying two days later on the third of August from Teterboro Airport in New Jersey, to Boston and as the estimated time en route will take approximately forty-two minutes, no catering will be required.

Leg 3 says that you will be leaving the third of August from Boston and will travel approximately **6.0 hours** to Burbank in California. This time there will be a total of five passengers and three crew, which brings the number of meals to eight, plus one extra, which equals **nine meals.** As the departure time out of Boston is 5.00 P.M. EST or 2100 hours Zulu, it would mean that you would serve cocktails with snacks (to the passengers only of course), and a full dinner only, and you, the flight attendant, will be responsible for designing the entire menu and ordering the catering.

The first step in designing a meal plan such as this is to go to your passenger profile lists (you should have them now from the first leg) and select the names of all the passengers. For the three new passengers you will need to call them, or someone associated with them, and find out their needs and work around the entire group of passengers and crew together. The final analysis should look something like this:

LEG 3

CATERER: Boston Elite Caterers
TEL: 898-567-XXXX
CONTACT: Mary

COCKTAIL SNACKS

1 Medium - antipasto platter with selection of Italian & Swiss cheese, Polish salami, pickles & olives
1 Medium - Vegetable crudite platter with assorted vegetables and dips.

MENU #1 – SEAFOOD MEDLEY – TOTAL = 7

SALAD
Caesar salad with garlic croutons and grated Parmesan cheese

MAIN COURSE
Australian lobster tail
King prawns
Scallops
Cracked Canadian crab claws

MENU # 2 – CHICKEN – TOTAL - 2

SALAD
Garden salad topped with champagne vinaigrette & shredded Parmesan

MAIN COURSE
Grilled marinated chicken breast with herbs
Steamed asparagus
Baby herbed carrots
Twice baked potatoes

DESSERTS – TOTAL - 9

Bavarian log
Pavalova with whipped cream, kiwi and strawberries

BEVERAGES

Choice of wine/champagne

DELIVERY TO AIRCRAFT. $10 SURCHARGE FOR EXTRA MILEAGE

Whenever placing an order for catering always get the person to read back what they have written and make sure they understand precisely what you want. Ask them if they will be the person making up the order as many times it will be given to someone else who does not interpret it the way it's supposed to be. This is a common problem overseas where there is a language barrier. I recall one flight attendant in Italy asking for some fresh dill and parsley – enough for twelve people, but what she got was a dozen large pots of herbs all ready to be planted in the garden. Yes, they were very fresh herbs indeed!

Also, take note of the season and weather you're flying in. Obviously hot soup is preferable to a cold salad in sub-zero temperatures and vichyssoise to hot chili in a heatwave. Finally, don't feel intimidated when placing an order. Ask the caterer for help when necessary as they usually have a lot of experience in their field. Mistakes and changes will happen, but if you keep a cool head, you can learn to improvise successfully. I remember when I was supposed to depart San Francisco for Los Angeles with two passengers and fourteen people showed up. Suddenly, the oversized donuts and pastries became mini platters of bite-sized petits fours, sprinkled with blueberries, and garnished with strawberries and edible flowers. Incredibly, there was some left over and everyone said they had a great time!

WHEN TO SERVE THE FOOD

The next step now is to determine when to serve the food. Unlike a restaurant, your times for providing meal service to your passengers will be calculated according to the position of the plane in the sky. If you are flying in a Gulfstream jet for example and using the Johnson Corporation Trip Sheet as a reference, then you would know that the length of the journey for leg 3 is six hours. During that six hours however, there is a twenty-minute climb to altitude and a twenty-minute decent to the approach and landing. This means that you have forty minutes less to work in the cruise portion of the flight, which means you have five hours and twenty minutes left to work in.

Time	6.00 Hours
Less	0.20 Minutes climb to altitude
Less	<u>0.20 Minutes descent to approach and landing</u>
TOTAL	<u>5.20 Minutes</u>

This is ample time to serve snacks and a full three-course meal; however, some trips may require two meals, such as a breakfast and lunch, within the same time. It takes careful planning to organize each leg so that on the trips that are less hectic you have time to do extra chores, such as cleaning cupboards and polishing silverware and glassware.

The leg 3 portion above would go something like this:

1. Serve beverages and snacks
2. Set and decorate tables
3. Prepare the food
4. Cook/warm the food
5. Serve the food
6. Give drink refills
7. Give second helpings
8. Final beverage refills
9. Clear the tables
10. Clean the galley
11. Prepare for landing

UNDERSTANDING GOURMET

When you first begin as a flight attendant you may encounter catering language that could be rather intimidating if you have not been exposed to it before. These "gourmet" expressions sound quite formal but, in fact, they are just fancy expressions for ordinary things. Let's take a look.

The basics of gourmet stem from French cuisine although it's not limited to French cooking. It simply means that the cook has a proficient knowledge of international cuisines and beverages, and can prepare and present them in an attractive and appetizing manner. It's the art of understanding how different foods and spices mix well together and how to artistically arrange it all on a plate so that it looks like a feast fit for a king.

The first step now is to understand the gourmet language. The following are words or terms you will hear frequently within the corporate aviation world and, in time, they will become part of your language, too.

GOURMET VOCABULARY

AGNEAU - lamb
ALMONDINE – made with almonds
APERITIF – pre-dinner drink
APPETIZER – small portions of food served before a main course
ASPIC - a dish that is covered in a flavored gelatin
AU GRATIN – dish topped with crumbs and cheese and then grilled
AU JUS – a dish served with its own juices; eg. roast beef
BABA GHANNOUGE – Mediterranean eggplant dip
BAGUETTE – long, thin bread
BASIL – herb used in entrees, soups and sauces
BEARNAISE – a sauce made out of egg yolks, white wine, shallots and butter
BECHAMEL SAUCE – thick white or cream sauce
BISQUE – Thick seafood and tomato soup made with cream and wine
BOUILLABAISSE – Mixed seafood dish flavored with tomatoes, onions and spices
BOUILLON – Broth obtained from meat – usually poultry or beef
BRIE- type of cheese named after the French region its from
BRINE CURED OLIVES – olives from Greece
BRIOCHE – cream filled sweet pastry
CAFÉ – coffee
CANAPE – an appetizer made of bread pieces with toppings
CAPERS – tangy, pickled buds used in salads and with seafood
CAPPUCCINO – espresso coffee mixed with milk and topped with cream
CAVIAR* – Sturgeon roe used as toppings for appetizers. Beluga is the most popular.
CHATEAUBRIAND – center of a beef fillet which usually serves two or more people
CHAUSSEUR – Stuffed mushrooms
COMPOTE – dessert of stewed fruit
CONSOMMÉ – strong beef bouillon often used in soups
COQUILLE – Scallops; eg. Coquilles St. Jacques
DIJON – spicy mustard named after the town its from
ÉCLAIR – sweet pastry filled with flavored creams or custard
ENTRÉE – main course
ESCARGOT – snails
FALAFEL – Mediterranean chickpea balls

FILLET – poultry, meat or fish with the bones removed
FILLO DOUGH – dough used in Middle Eastern baking
FOIE GRAS – type of pate made from duck or goose liver
FRICASSEE – white meat sautéed in wine and served with white sauce
GAME – meat from wild animals or birds
HUMMUS – Garbanzo bean sauce
HOISON SAUCE – Chinese sauce made from soybean and pepper
HOLLANDAISE – butter sauce made with egg yolks, wine and vinegar
HORS D'OEUVRE – an appetizer usually served on toothpicks or sticks
JULIENNE – vegetables that are cut into small strips
KEBABS – meat, seafood and vegetables which are skewered and cooked over a flame
KOSHER – food prepared according to Jewish law
LEGUME – a pod vegetable such as a pea
LIQUEUR – strong, alcoholic beverage
MARINADE – A mix that meat is soaked in to increase flavor
MEDALLION – round or oval slices of meat often called tournedos
MIGNON – Meat cut from the tenderloin and when boned is called filet mignon
MINESTRONE – thick vegetable soup with added potatoes and tomatoes
MOUSSE - cold soufflé dessert
NAPOLEON – sweet, layered custard pastry
NAVARIN – mutton or lamb stew
NOISETTE – small, round medallion of lamb or veal
PATE – an appetizer made from goose or duck livers
PESTO – Italian sauce made from pine nuts
PETITE – small, little
PILAF – seasoned rice
POLENTA – Italian cornmeal
PRIMAVERA – Italian for spring vegetables
PRIME RIB – meat cut from the forequarters
PROSCIUTTO – deli style dried Italian ham
PUREE – mashed or blended into a pulp or thick juice
QUAIL – small bird
QUICHE – savory pie containing eggs, bacon and cheese
RATATOUILLE – stew made of eggplant, tomatoes and zucchinis
ROULADE – vegetables wrapped in cold sliced meat
SALISBURY STEAK – ground beefsteak covered with sauce
SAUTÉ – brown food in a pan of hot butter or oil
SCAMPI – fried prawns in garlic
SHALLOTS – a garlic onion cross
TABOULI – Bulgar wheat salad
TART – small pie
TARTAR SAUCE – sauce used mainly for fish
TORTE – Large multilayered cake with rich, sweet fillings
TRUFFLES – type of fungi considered to be a delicacy
VEAL – calf meat
VENISON – deer meat
VICHYSSOISE – cold soup made of leeks and potatoes
VOL-AU-VENT – small hollow pastry shell stuffed with seasonings

*CAVIAR

Caviar simply means fish eggs, and the better quality type comes from the Beluga sturgeon. Cheaper types come from salmon, lumpfish and whitefish. The type of fish determines the color of the roe (eggs). Once a caviar container is opened it must be refrigerated and preferably used as soon as possible. Caviar can be eaten directly, or used as a garnish, which always adds a colorful, luxurious touch. It should always be served well chilled and placed on a bed of crushed ice, with small spoons of ivory, bone, or if unavoidable, plastic. Never use metal spoons, as the metal will interfere with its flavor. Accompaniments can include crackers, cream cheese, toast slices and chopped eggs. Beverages should be non-sweet. Extra dry champagne, chardonnay and vodka are the most popular and the most suitable beverages to use.

SAMPLE MENUS

BREAKFAST
Fresh fruit cup
3-egg omelet with filling of your choice
Muffins, toast
Juice
Coffee/tea

LUNCH
Garden salad with vegetable florets
Grilled marinated chicken breast
Rice risotto
Fresh fruit
Chocolate truffles
Choice of wine/champagne
Coffee/tea

DINNER
Grilled salmon with lemon
Red blush potatoes seasoned with rosemary
Steamed asparagus
Petite pastries
Choice of wine/champagne

****

BREAKFAST
Cold cereal
Fruit yogurt
Danish
Fresh fruit
Juice
Coffee/tea

LUNCH
New York deli sandwich (choice of bread and meat)
Fresh fruit compote
Russian sorbet
Choice of wine/champagne
Coffee/tea

DINNER
Garden salad with champagne vinaigrette and shredded Parmesan
Scallopine of filet mignon Marsala
Baby herbed carrots
Twice baked potatoes
Fresh berry medley
Choice of wine/champagne
Coffee/tea

SAMPLE MENUS

BUFFET BREAKFAST PLATTERS
- Smoked Norwegian salmon tray with capers, chopped onion, cream cheese, bagels, Hebrew bread
- Pastry tray with selection of petite pastries, muffins, toast, assorted honey and jams

BOXED LUNCH #1 (REGULAR)
Chef's salad
Imported cheeses with assorted crackers
Grape clusters
Cold beef tenderloin with horseradish sauce
New York cheesecake
Choice of beverage

BOXED LUNCH #2 (GOURMET)
Pate de foie gras with garlic toast points
Chilled avocado soup
Stuffed sliced quail with sauce chasseur
Assorted fresh berries
Chocolate truffles
Choice of beverage

BOXED LUNCH #3 (MEDITERRANEAN)
Tabouli
Falafel
Potato salad
Hummus sauce
Baba Ghannouge (eggplant) dip
Pita bread
Melon balls

MID-MORNING SNACK TRAYS
- Fresh sliced/sculptured fruit tray with assorted berries, tropical fruits and dipping sauces
- Assorted Italian and American mini sandwiches, with Hye Rollers and American crackers and cheese

MID-AFTERNOON SNACK TRAYS
- Antipasto platter with selection of Italian and Swiss cheeses, Italian and Polish salami, pickles, olives, assorted crackers and bread
- Vegetable crudite platter with ten assorted fresh vegetables and assorted dips

AFTER-DINNER SNACK TRAYS
- Petite pastries with assorted chocolates and candies
- Sliced fresh fruit medley
- Dried fruit and nut medley

TIPS FOR ORDERING AND BUYING FOOD

SAUCES

When placing an order ask the caterer to put the sauces in separate sealed containers. Add the sauces when you are ready to serve the food because foods such as salad and fruit will become soggy if sauce mix is placed on them for any length of time. When the catering arrives, make sure that all the containers are tightly sealed. You will certainly appreciate this when your platters lurch sideways as the plane accelerates rapidly as it climbs to altitude. Also check the passenger profile lists to see if liquors and other alcoholic beverages can be added to sauce mixes. Those who refrain from consuming alcohol should feel free to eat without questioning the ingredients.

FRUIT

When ordering fruit ask the caterer to peel, slice, dice, chop or sculpture the fruit into pieces small enough to eat without too much difficulty, and to remove all stones, pits and seeds. This also applies to dried fruit such as prunes, apricot and dates.

SEAFOOD

When requesting seafood ask the caterer to crack the shells of crabs and lobsters so that they can be eaten easily with a fork. Request that prawns have the heads and the vein from their backs removed. Also ask for fillet (without the bones) in every type of fish dish.

GARNISHMENTS

When ordering or buying garnishments select those that blend in with the food type and are edible and fresh. Color highlights a meal so look for garnishments that will help to give this look. Use sculptured vegetables and fruit as containers for other foods, such as green and red pepper cases filled with potato salad, or tomato cases stuffed with coleslaw.

NOTE: Learning how to sculpture garnishments correctly will add beauty to your meals and tantalize the passengers' taste buds. Check the Internet or your local bookstore for foods on this subject as it really does make a difference.

UNDERSTANDING WINES

Wine has been with civilization since the beginning of time and fortunately today it's still one of those pleasures in life that you don't have to know much about to enjoy. Of course vintners and critics have a higher discriminating taste in the multiple facets of wine production; however, for most of us, it's much more simple. When taken in moderation, wine, like everything else, is a wonderful complement to a healthful style of living; however, keep in mind that the wine (or any alcohol) motto on board an aircraft should be "less is best." Alcohol consumption causes dehydration and too much causes intoxication hence the advice.

Most corporate flight attendants are required to serve alcoholic beverages as part of their job. If you are a non-drinker or have limited exposure to fine wines it doesn't matter because the information on these pages should be enough to help you buy, order, and finally, serve the wine with confidence.

WINE VOCABULARY

A.O.C. – Appellation d'Origine Controlee. A French law covering the entire process of wine making
AROMA – The smell of a particular grape in a wine
BEAUJOLAIS - a light, fruity, red Burgundy wine
BODY – a taste of fullness in the body of a wine
BORDEAUX – any of various wines produced in the region surrounding Bordeaux, France
BOUQUET – the wine's aroma heightened by age
BRUT CHAMPAGNE – unsweetened or dry
CABERNET – dry red wine
CHABLIS - dry white wine from the Burgundy region of France
CHAMPAGNE – famous sparkling wine from the province of Champagne in France
CHARDONNAY – dry white wine – usually the most expensive
CHENIN BLANC – white wine
CHIANTI – a basic red wine
CLARET – dry red wine
DEMI-SEC – sweet wine, a good dessert wine
DOM PERIGNON – sparkling wine named after Benedictine monk, a premium champagne
DRY WINE – a wine in which most or all of its sugar has been removed by fermentation
EXTRA SEC –means extra dry but is actually slightly sweet
GEWURZTRAMINER- a rich, spicy white wine
LEGS – Formation of wine on the inside of a glass
MERLOT – red wine
PINOT BLANC – white wine made from white Pinot grapes
PINOT NOIR – red wine made from purple Pinot grapes
POUILLY FUISSE – high-quality dry white wine from Burgundy, France
POUILLY FUME – dry white wine from the Loire Valley of France
RIESLING – fine white wine
SAUTERNES – sweet, white wine
SAUVIGNON BLANC – dry white wine from France or California from this grape
SEC – means dry in French but is actually quite a sweet wine
SPARKLING WINE – a sparkling wine (can only be called Champagne if it comes from there).
TANNIN – A bitter substance that preserves old wines but disappears upon maturity
VINS DE TABLE – French table wine
VINTAGE – More commonly means a grape crop from a particular year

NOTE: The wines listed here are either named after the regions or the type of grape they come from in France.

CATEGORIES OF FRENCH WINES:

French wines are divided into four categories:

1. **Appellation d'Origine Controlee (AOC)**
   These are the best French wines available. They are produced under meticulous conditions and heavily regulated in the way the grapes are grown, the type of grape used and in the alcoholic content.

2. **Vins de Qualite Superieur (VDQS)**
   These are superior wines that rank just below the AOC wines.

3. **Vins de Pays**
   These are country wines ranking below the VDQS.

4. **Vins de Table**
   These are the most common table wines used by the people in France.

To determine which category French wine fits into look for any of the words mentioned above written above or below the label. If your passengers are connoisseurs of fine French wine then you would buy wines in the number-one AOC category. If they are content with a "house wine" as it's called in America then you would buy wines from the number-four Vins de Table category. A good point to remember is that just because it's French, doesn't mean to say it's the best. The United States has some superb wines along with many other countries such as Australia and South America, so when buying, the right choice is to buy what your passengers like best.

BOTTLE SIZES

SPLIT	6.5 ounces
HALF BOTTLE	13 ounces
BOTTLE	26 ounces
MAGNUM	52 ounces

TIPS ON BUYING WINE

The best advice is to visit the local wine merchant in your area to familiarize yourself with all areas of wine purchasing and to learn how to select the appropriate wines to go with the meals without spending a fortune. In selecting a wine merchant make sure when you enter the establishment that they are an expert and not just a salesperson. You can determine this by observing the way the wine is stacked. Is it standing erect or on its side? Is it in the window getting heated in the sun, or is it keeping cool in an air-conditioned room? Does the merchant swing a bottle from its neck or is it removed gently from the shelf to prevent sediment disturbance. Obviously a wine merchant who loves and cares about wine is going to be much more help to you when planning your catering. Of course the true test will come from your passengers' response as they will usually tell you their opinion of the wine.

To reduce your time shopping and to get better discounts, buy your wine in bulk. When you do, find an area such as a hangar where it can be stored in a cool, dark place where the temperature does not exceed fifty-five degrees Fahrenheit. Also make sure that it won't be exposed to movement, draft or temperature changes. Although your wine may arrive in boxes, unless you can turn the boxes on their sides, remove the bottles and place them horizontally on a rack so that their corks stay wet, thus preventing any air from entering in. This will help the wine to age properly until it's ready to be served.

LIQUOR

Usually, liquor on board a plane is limited to five main types: scotch, whiskey, vodka, gin and rum. Often they will be on display in decanters located somewhere in the galley area. If you are the one to originate the purchase then buy the best quality liquor you can get. Cheap liquor can never be concealed no matter how much is poured or added into it.

Quite often, someone will purchase the alcohol other than the flight attendant. When this happens make a note of the type of alcohol, brand, vintage, and from whom, and where it was purchased. Keep this information in your files for reference in the event that you're the one who is responsible sometime in the future.

MIXED DRINKS

You must learn how to mix drinks correctly. Most drinks requested on board are for the common mixes such as gin and tonic, vodka and orange juice or Bacardi and Coke. Occasionally, you will be asked to make a fancier concoction such as a flavored Margarita or a Bloody Mary and if you are unfamiliar with these then you will need to purchase a Bar Guide (book or mini-computer), which explains clearly how to mix them. Many mixed drinks require extra accessories such as fluted umbrellas, or pickled onions and olives on a stick to enhance their appearance. If you are unfamiliar with any of these then I would advise you to study the pictures in your Bar book/computer and learn how to copy them. If you follow the recipes exactly and add the right garnishments, you will find that even if you are a non-drinker, making a mixed drink is really very easy.

BAR SNACKS

The salty versions such as nuts and pretzels should be used sparingly as high altitude creates natural expansion of the body. Excessive salt can cause fluid retention problems, especially in the ankles, because of the prolonged sitting. Nuts are also high fiber and at high altitude can create excessive stomach distention and bloating resulting in severe pain. Order or buy snacks that are both low in fiber and sodium and you will have much happier, healthier passengers.

INTOXICATED/PROBLEM PASSENGERS

I have included "problem passengers" in this section because it's usually a problem related to alcohol consumption. A smart flight attendant does not allow this to happen by learning a few simple rules:

1. Pour the first or second drink the correct strength and then gradually weaken them until there is no alcohol in the mix. If it's wine, take your time refilling the glass.

2. Camouflage the fake drinks with lots of decorations such as fluted umbrellas, large cocktail onions, etc.

3. Distract their drinking attention by adding glasses of water, snacks, and entertainment.

4. Turn up the heat a little to make them drowsy.

5. Notify the Pilot-In-Command if there's a problem or if the situation deteriorates.

NOTE: Some of your passengers will arrive at the plane already drunk. Never underestimate the seriousness of this and advise the Pilot-In-Command immediately. It's the PIC's responsibility to make the decision if the passenger/s will be able to fly, or if the trip should continue. Unfortunately, if it's your boss, you may have to change jobs.

CHAPTER 9: PREPARING YOUR PLANE FOR FLIGHT

Most corporate aircraft can be divided into four main areas that you will be responsible for in ensuring the comfort and safety of your passengers. They are the cabin, galley, lavatories and baggage compartment. In some of the larger jets there are bedroom suites and a host of other amenities; however, the probability is that you will start off in something much smaller, so in this chapter we will briefly look at some of the main points in each of the areas of a smaller jet that you need to know.

THE CABIN

TABLEWARE

One of the skills you should really excel in is setting a beautiful table. Learn how to master this and you will have a lot of happy days flying. Everybody loves a beautifully set table and somehow, even if the food is not that good, a magnificent table setting can offset that. You may not have any choice in the type of dinnerware, silverware or linens that are on board, but whether you like them or not it's your job to make it all look spectacular. In some cases you may have to resort to napkin origami, but if it works, just do it!

PLACEMATS
Always use placemats if tablecloths are not available. Most often the tables are made of expensive materials and food or beverage spills can be costly to repair. If you have a choice in purchasing the placemats, buy the heavier, larger type with a non-slip base. Avoid fringes and frills around the edges that can catch on silverware or tip glasses over.

NAPKIN RINGS
Buy good quality, assorted types and alternate them with the meals you serve. This adds variety and individual style to each meal setting.

NAPKINS
Always give your passengers napkins when food or beverages are served. Paper cocktail napkins are quite suitable to use with drinks; however, at meal time it is preferable to use oversized material ones. One tip is to place two large napkins inside each other at each place setting. This can be done by folding one napkin of a different color, inside the other. This not only provides extra color, but also gives the passengers more protection for their clothing as well as the furnishings around them. During the meal always check to see if new ones are needed. On a bumpy flight they may go through quite a few.

Some napkins have metallic threads through them, which makes them difficult to dry-clean. Read the labels carefully. Do not give them this type when serving food or beverages such as pasta and red wine as they will stain easily. They cannot be bleached and chemical agents may destroy them completely. White napkins are best because they can be bleached and used for multiple functions such as lining breadbaskets or covering platters.

DINNERWARE
An important point to remember with all the dinnerware you use is to check the labels on the base of the plates. Many are painted in gold and other precious metals and cannot be placed in a microwave or dishwasher.

On a long journey you will need to ensure that you will have enough dinnerware for each of the meals as you will have no way to clean those that have been used because of the limited washing facilities on board. Also, there will be no dishwasher and limited water supplies. Many sinks are tiny, approximately half the size of a home sink, and are frequently coated in gold for decorative appearances which makes washing dishes out of the question. You will usually wash them once you land at the next airport terminal.

SILVERWARE

Quite often it's just that – solid silver! Great care must be taken not to scratch the surfaces and to keep them highly polished. This applies to all types of silverware. In cleaning, check if they can be cleaned in a dishwasher, as the heating cycle may damage the metal coating.

GLASSWARE

Stemmed glassware is the most difficult of all the items used as they are fragile and tip easily. More damage is done to a cabin's interior with glassware spills and breakages than in any other way. If the passengers are drinking alcohol then the problem is compounded, so be alert and ready!

Most stemware has to be cleaned by hand because of its fragility. After cleaning, hold the glass up to the light to make sure that all stains and marks have been removed. Dry them with a towel as glasses left to dry by themselves will inevitably show a cloudy film and water marks.

FLOWERS

Try to have some sort of floral arrangement with each meal. Fresh daisies, orchids, carnations or delicate rosebuds add color and beauty to any meal setting. Place edible flowers on your fruits and berries and be generous with them on your platters. When placing flowers on top of food, always wash them with a gentle spray to eliminate any contaminants that may be on them. If it's a special occasion, such as a birthday, you may want to give the person a corsage as well.

For decorative purposes within the cabin, avoid flowers with high perfumes or those that can produce allergies such as lilies and arrange them in heavy-durable vases that won't slip or slide easily, or cause water damage if they fall over.

SERVING TRAYS, BASKETS AND PLATTERS

These can greatly enhance the food you serve. Use colored doilies in white, gold or silver, or drape grapes over the edges to give them that luxury look. Throw out chipped or cracked platters, or any that are visibly stained. These are your showpieces and should look spectacular along with the food that you serve.

NOTE: Always remember when serving food that the plane is in constant motion in the air and as a result, anything placed on a surface has the ability to move. This means great care must be taken to minimize the chances of spills and accidents from occurring.

LINEN AND BEDDING

LAP BLANKETS

The main point to remember when purchasing lap blankets is that some cashmeres and wool blankets shed a lot of fluff and adhere to the passengers' clothing, especially men's dark suits. Also, blankets with tassels and fringes can be a hazard to passengers with shoe heels, such as ladies stilettos. It is preferable to buy blankets that have plain sewn edges instead.

PILLOWS

Every seat on the plane should have a small pillow for traveling to aid in the passenger's comfort. Full-sized pillows can be kept in airtight, dust-free containers in the baggage compartment where they can be reached upon request. When buying pillows, opt for the hypo-allergenic ones that can be dry-cleaned and make sure the pillow cases are cleaned and replaced after each use.

SHEETS

Cotton is best for use within a cabin environment because it is a natural fiber and allows the body to breathe easily. Cotton is also a lot hardier than silk

TELEVISION/ENTERTAINMENT SYSTEMS

In general, most new aircraft use high-resolution, flat-screen **televisions**. They provide superior picture quality, are lighter, and require less in engineering costs to install them.

The latest **entertainment systems** are integrated by a central digital control system computer. With this system, switches throughout the aircraft can control all the entertainment functions at each seat. At the present time these systems are very expensive and so are not available on many aircraft. The most common systems are hard-wired together and usually require some instruction and practice as to how they function. Most of the television and entertainment systems can be controlled by remote control now; however, because the systems differ on various planes you must refer to the manuals and the rest of the crew for proper instruction regarding their usage.

NOTE: There are now digital control systems that allow you to control the position of the shades throughout the aircraft along with the entertainment system. These are becoming increasingly popular.

TELEPHONES

There are three main types of in-flight telephones:

1. **SKYPHONE:** This is an analog system that is limited to line of sight in the continental USA only and unfortunately, has many non-service areas.

- **MAGNESTAR:** This is a digital system limited to the continental USA only. This is the most popular because of its cost and clarity, and almost complete coverage.

2. **SATCOM:** This is the means of communicating around the world via satellites. The antennas of an aircraft are controlled by a computer that is linked to the aircraft's navigation system so they are always pointing to an active satellite somewhere in the world. Although the system is expensive, it's the best way to communicate.

There are also other systems that are used by the pilots, for example:

- HF radio – (High Frequency radio). This is great if the pilots can spare a radio to monitor certain frequencies.

- AFIS – (Airborne Flight Information System). This works via VHF ground stations and satellites in orbit around the world. This system allows the pilots to send and receive text messages to and from the aircraft, plus get weather information, flight plans and other operations data. This is the most popular system because it is relatively inexpensive compared to the other forms of communication and very reliable.

Communication is important for the crew and passengers and as a result, whatever is available on board is used often. Make sure you understand how all the connections work.

EMERGENCY EQUIPMENT

You will learn extensively about the types of emergency equipment and how to use it in your formal training. It is extremely important that you fully understand how to use all the equipment and how to react and cope in an emergency situation. Remember that each aircraft is different and so you will need to apply the instruction you receive to the type of aircraft you will eventually be flying in.

Most aircraft will have many of the following on board for use in emergency situations:

Crash Axe
Escape Slides
Fire Extinguishers
First Aid Kit
Flashlights
Flotation Cushions
Life Jackets
Life Rafts
Smoke Hoods
Survival Kits
Survival Suits

Escape slides, like those on an airline, are normally found on the larger jets and so it is probable that most of you will not be using them. Regardless, heed the instruction given carefully, because a few companies have upgraded their small planes to larger ones with escape slides. There are also various styles and designs in flotation jackets, life rafts and flotation cushions, so be aware of how each one operates. Once you are hired as a flight attendant, you can ask the rest of the flight crew to help you familiarize yourself with all the emergency equipment on board your plane.

There are four main types of fire extinguishers including carbon dioxide, dry chemical, Halon and water, however, the type of extinguisher you use will depend on the type of fire that has occurred. Fires can result from the electrical systems, baggage, galley (usually cooking equipment), lavatory (usually from cigarettes), entertainment systems, lighting and so on.

Always be aware that the FAA expects you to fully comprehend how to take the correct and immediate action during a fire emergency. You will probably not be able to rely on the pilots because they will be busy preparing for an emergency landing. As you can see the instruction you receive from your training will have a great impact on the lives of all those on board and the success or failure of the emergency situation may rest with you.

THE GALLEY

APPLIANCES

One of the mysteries in galley designs is why microwave ovens are so often placed at ground level instead of bench level. As a result many flight attendants spend hours on their knees or bending down to reach an oven that's in a ridiculous place. Well, we could blame the designers, but that won't solve the problem. The fact is, you have to work with it and be extra cautious to guard against fires because it's difficult to watch how it's cooking when it's located at your feet.

Before you use any of the appliances on-board read the instruction manuals or ask other crew members to ensure that you are using them correctly. A large number of on-board fires have resulted from crewmembers not fully understanding the requirements of the cooking equipment.

MICROWAVE OVENS

This is perhaps the most common type of cooking appliance on an aircraft. They are popular because they have the ability to do multiple functions including defrosting, heating, warming and cooking in rapid time. Another benefit is that you can use disposable paper containers that do not require cleaning afterward, thereby saving time and the limited water supply. It is preferable to cook foods in crockery containers or certain paper products as some of the plastic containers have been known to transfer chemicals from the plastic into the food.

Never place any dishware or container that has metal such as gold and silver on its surface, or contains aluminum foil, as the electromagnetic waves may cause more than sparks to fly!

CONVECTION OVENS

Although a convection oven looks like a microwave oven, there is quite a disparity between the two, so make sure you understand what's in your galley. A convection oven cooks slower than a microwave, but is faster than a conventional oven. One advantage of this type over a microwave is its ability to brown or roast foods to a better, crispier quality and foods can be left in to keep warm. The advantage over a conventional oven is that it's smaller and can fit into a compact space.

ADDITIONAL

COFFEE POTS

Coffee drinkers usually have a passion for drinking it so learn how to make a good pot. Most air terminals will offer you free coffee as part of their service for your plane being there; however, no matter how good it may look, avoid their kind offer. Rarely do they have the time to make a fresh pot just before you leave, and then even if they do, it could be an hour or two before your passengers decide they want it. By then the three fundamental basics of a good cup of coffee - flavor, body and acidity, have changed. Instead, make the coffee yourself shortly before it's required.

If you use coffee beans, make sure you read the label to determine the right grind for your type of coffee-maker. No matter where you are, always use bottled water as it's filtered and free of various flavors. When the last drop of water has flowed through, swirl or stir the pot gently so that the richer sediment on the bottom will mix with the weaker portion on top, and then serve as soon as possible. If not, transfer it to a coffee thermos flask immediately.

If you are purchasing one, look for the automatic drip version that allows you to set the time and have it brewing and ready for the right moment. Newer versions now also have a gold-coated filter basket that eliminates filter paper. If you buy one of these baskets, do not put it in the dishwasher because the heat will destroy the coating. Instead, rinse it gently with mild soap and water and allow it to dry.

REFRIGERATOR/ICE DRAWERS

This seems to be another problem area in a galley because there just isn't room for one the right size. If there is one, it's usually small with two shelves, scarcely enough to hold meals for a lot of passengers. Often there is an ice drawer as well where food can be stored. Many flight attendants take along ice chests, filled with ice to use for additional cold storage. This is an excellent idea because once the ice chest has served its purpose it can be used again for storage of something else.

FOOD STORAGE

Due to the limited refrigeration and storage facilities on board, food poisoning is a serious concern. To help prevent this from happening all food whether packaged, canned or fresh, should be in air-tight containers and replaced frequently. Opened packages should either be placed in sealed containers or discarded after use. Cold food should be stored at minus 40 degrees Fahrenheit and hot foods should be stored at no less than 140 degrees Fahrenheit.

In preparing the cabin for a trip make sure that all the interior storage areas are cleaned and sterilized and that fresh supplies are added on a regular basis. Don't use the expiration dates on packages as a guide but instead, consider the weather and temperature conditions your plane has been waiting in while out on the ramp. Heat dries out food rapidly and within days, the food can become quite stale. If in doubt – toss it out!

THE LAVATORY/BATHROOM

Along with the lavatory, this area usually consists of a sink with washing facilities, vanity drawers and mirrors, plus garment racks. At the beginning of each flight the lavatory should be inspected to see if it contains water and chemicals. Disposable toilet tissue, available from camping and recreational stores, should be used in preference to regular toilet paper, because it reduces the chances of clogging the drains. At the end of each flight the terminal crew should service it for you; however, don't take it for granted that they have. Check before you leave the plane that it has been done and check again before you leave on a trip that it's still operational.

NOTE: This is one area of the plane that is highly susceptible to fires from people smoking and so it's strongly recommended that you make frequent trips into this area to check places such as the ashtrays (if there are any) and the trash can. Don't assume that people will always observe the non-smoking signs. This area is also susceptible to flooding when passengers leave the water tap on so constant surveillance must be observed.

When stocking the cabinets, use the aircraft supplies list as a reference and fill them with all the necessities making sure that everything is new and unopened, especially the medicines. Place fresh, clean towels in, or on, the receptacles and new unopened soaps in the soap dish. Incidentally, the best type of hand soap to use is the hand-pump type as it can be used hygienically over and over again

BAGGAGE COMPARTMENT

WATER TANKS

The water tanks are usually contained in the rear of the plane near the baggage compartment. The mechanics or pilots may be the ones who service them for you, but you should know how to do this yourself. There are many types of water tanks so check with the Pilot-In-Command for its operation. All water tanks should be filled and checked before each flight.

NOTE: On overseas flights there will be some countries where you will not be able to use their water because of contamination. This will require you to conserve the water in the tanks carefully and carry extra supplies. Also, in sub-zero temperatures the water tanks and the entire A/C water system must be drained to avoid freezing and damage to the system.

BAGGAGE RACKS

Space is limited in the baggage compartment and is reduced even more when there are lots of passenger luggage and extra supplies being carried for overseas trips. Avoid cluttering this area with items that are not required for each trip.

CHAPTER 10: THE FLIGHT DAY HAS ARRIVED

WHEN TO START WORK

Two hours before departure is the time most flight crews are generally expected to turn up for work on the day of a trip. In the beginning, you may want to go earlier so that you will have more time to prepare the meals, especially if there are going to be a lot of passengers.

ORGANIZING THE CATERING

During this time your catering should be on its way or have arrived. You should also have made arrangements to obtain any additional items not ordered from the caterers. If you are staying at a hotel, keep the copy of the newspaper they deliver to your room and ask the crew to do the same, as you will need more than one copy if there are multiple passengers. This could save you a lot of hassle trying to find a convenience store in a different city.

FINAL CHECK THROUGH THE PLANE

Starting from the red carpet at the entrance to the plane, begin your walk-thru. Shake or remove any dust or dirt from the carpet and stairway. Polish or shine the handrails leading up to the front entrance. The overhead light in the entranceway should be on, likewise all soft lighting throughout the cabin, regardless of the time of day. The carpets should have been vacuumed, all the furnishings and windows cleaned and polished, and ceilings and seats wiped or brushed to give that fresh look. Magazines and newspapers should be placed on a front table, along with any flower arrangements. It's a good idea to remove all the loose advertising cards from inside the magazines so that they won't end up littering the floor later. A pillow and lap blanket can be placed on, or near each seat, along with the company brochure detailing the trip if required. Air-sick bags and briefing cards should also be placed at each seat. Any music should be kept soft and low and be of the company's or passengers' choice.

The galley and lavatory areas should be spotless – there is no exception to the rule. In the galley, dishes, glasses and cutlery should all be cleaned and ready for use. Food supplies should be correctly stored and the catering (if it has arrived) placed in a secure position in the correct storage areas. Once again, check that lids and seals on any liquid containers are tightly closed and that once placed into the appropriate storage areas, they cannot move. Remember that soon you will be taking off at high speed down a runway and climbing at a sharp angle of ascent, so anything not packed properly will move and probably suffer damage.

In the bathroom/lavatory areas check that water and chemicals have been placed in the lavatory and that it has been cleaned and is operable. Open cupboards and ensure that all supplies have been replaced and plenty of fresh towels are available, along with toilet rolls, making sure you have plenty of spares. Also, empty any trash and leave the light on.

In the rear of the plane check that the water tanks have been filled and that the baggage compartment is ready for receiving the passengers' baggage.

This is also a good time to check with the pilots on weather and flying conditions and if any turbulence is expected en route. Find out if they need anything else in the cockpit other than bottled water and then sit back, relax and wait for your big moment, which seems to take forever the first time.

SPECIAL SECURITY

There may be times when extra security will be required to escort passengers. Political figures such as former American Presidents are assigned Secret Service agents to protect them for life. Once you receive notification that you will be flying a President, the Secret Service will arrive at your plane a few hours before departure. There they will thoroughly check the exterior and the interior of the plane, plus the surrounding area for anything considered a hazard. Dogs also will be brought on the plane to sniff for drugs, bombs or anything else. For this reason you must cooperate fully with all those in charge of their protection because the lives of everyone on board, including yourself, could be at risk.

The Secret Service agents are in constant communication with each other while the President and others are en route to your plane. They will advise you the exact minute when the President will appear and once you get this information you should be waiting in place by the red carpet for their arrival. Be prepared for the press, television crews and fans to be present. Often the President and others will stop to greet and meet the people, so try to remain out of the way and as inconspicuous as possible. Remember, it's their day – not yours.

Although you may be surrounded by Secret Service and police, always remain alert for breaches of security. Quickly and quietly, at the right time, help to get your passengers on board with a minimum of fuss and let the main ones choose where they want to sit, before the others take their place.

Always try to establish a professional rapport and let them have their privacy as best you can. If you have any questions you may want to ask the Secret Service for advice first, before disturbing the President. I have found that once you get to know them, after a while you will realize how truly blessed America has been and how lucky you are to be in their company - beyond the red carpet.

HOW TO ADDRESS THEM PROPERLY

There's a high probability that many of your passengers will have a title and so you should show respect and call them by their official title unless you are advised to do otherwise. The list below will help you to address them correctly.

TITLE	CORRECT ADDRESS
President of the United States	President –plus last name for example, Cavanagh
President's wife	Mrs. Cavanagh
Vice President	Mr. Brown
Vice President's wife	Mrs. Brown
Senator	Senator - plus last name
Governor	Governor - plus last name
Mayor	Mayor – plus last name
Judge	Your Honor
Priest	Father – plus his last name
Military personnel	By their rank – Captain, Brigadier plus their last name

PRE-BOARDING

"Showtime!" This is a common expression among flight crew. It simply means that one of the crew has spotted the passengers arriving and it's time for you to meet them. Remember now, how you present yourself in these early stages can set the pace for the entire journey and maybe a lot longer.

Before they even reach your plane you should be down at the bottom of the stairs standing by the red carpet eagerly awaiting their arrival. Be happy to see them; after all, they're the ones who make you a flight attendant. Introduce yourself and make them feel welcome at this time and personally escort them up the stairs if necessary. Often they come laden with countless bags, packages, gifts, food, sporting goods, boxes of wine and more. Ask them what needs to go into the cabin and what can be kept in the baggage compartment. If it's raining, carry a large umbrella to protect them and their belongings.

ON BOARD

Once they are inside, assist them with their hats, coats and anything else at this time. Perhaps they need a cool drink of water, or a moist, hot or cold face towel, or perhaps just someone to talk to. Listen to them – even to the children and don't forget to pat the pet – if you can.

LOADING THE BAGGAGE

Once everyone is settled, proceed to the rear of the plane and assist the pilots loading the baggage. Familiarize yourself with which bag belongs to which passenger because often you will be asked to retrieve one during the journey. If bags are passed to you unfolded, then don't fold them. They probably contain dress clothes that need to be hung on a garment rack to prevent wrinkling. Place them in an area where they can be reached by their owners during the course of the journey as some of them will change before they land. Be extra careful of furs and beaded silk garments, which can be easily damaged. Place them in an area where they will be least disturbed. Once all the bags are packed, secure them completely and close the rear hatch door from which they were passed through, making sure this is completely sealed and secured.

Note: The golden rule is never, ever, go into anyone's baggage unless asked to do so by the owner, or security police and then, only do it in their presence. You never want to be accused of a crime you didn't commit.

READY FOR TAKEOFF

Return to the passenger section and proceed with the emergency briefings, making sure that everyone is comfortable with the procedures. If not, give them individual instruction and if you have a briefing card, go through it with them. In an emergency a lot of panic can be reduced when passengers know what to do and how to help others. Make sure they understand how to operate all the emergency exits and especially, how to get out through a porthole window quickly in the event of a mishap.

You may also wish to brief everyone at this time (by referring to your beautifully designed welcome aboard booklets), on what they can expect on the journey as far as meals, entertainment, times, weather conditions, and so on, as well as familiarizing them with the amenities on board including the bathroom facilities. This is also a good time to look for fearful flyers. Usually, they will be extremely tense and maybe even fidgety as the time for takeoff draws nearer. If your efforts to calm them down fail, then sit beside them on takeoff to give them that added security. They will really appreciate it!

Once everyone is seated, do a final walk through the cabin. Check that all doors and cupboards are closed and locked, tables and seats are secured, front and rear entrances are closed and the passengers are ready with seatbelts and headrests in place. Remove magazines and newspapers, flower arrangements, etc., until a straight and level flight has been maintained. Also re-check that pets are secured. Finally, notify the Pilot-In-Command that the cabin is ready for takeoff and then take your seat and enjoy the first stage.

DEPARTURE CHECKLIST

- Water tanks filled; lavatories serviced
- Catering/supplies secure and ready
- Coffee pot and thermos secure and ready
- Circuit breakers checked*
- Doors, cupboards locked or secured
- All external exits, including baggage door, locked and secure
- Baggage secure
- Moveable items stowed
- Passengers' seatbelts on, seats erect and in position.
- Passengers briefed on all emergency procedures, events of journey
- Pets secure
- Advise Pilot-In-Command that the cabin is ready for takeoff
- Take your seat
- Bon voyage!

*The circuit breakers are usually located in the galley area and should be checked that they are all in. They connect various appliances and units to the electrical sources within the aircraft and will pop out when a circuit is overloaded or not functioning properly. Refer any problems to the Pilot-In-Command as soon as possible. Do not reset a circuit breaker more than twice. If it stills pops out then leave it out and have the maintenance crew check the circuit on the ground once the flight is over.

PART THREE: DURING THE FLIGHT

CHAPTER 11: SERVICE, SERVICE, SERVICE

This chapter is designed to guide you through the basics of taking care of your passengers while they're on board. Your aim is to serve them so incredibly well that they will feel as if it's the best journey they have ever had. The good news is that it's not hard to do in a private jet surrounded by all that luxury; however, there are certain key factors that can help make it just that much better.

The golden rule to making a trip spectacular is – service, service, service! In chapter one you were given all the basic requirements to becoming a successful corporate flight attendant and if you look closely, you will find a lot of them relate to service. Now, the secret behind such great service is a genuine love and desire to want to serve others because, without that passion, your service is merely adequate. You will be nothing more than a robotic flight attendant who just gets the job done.

The message is quite clear – if you don't have that genuine desire to serve others from the depths of your heart then don't consider working in this position. Once jet lag sets in and your time clock gets out of whack, serving others will become a chore not a passion. A good test is to ask yourself this question: "If money were no object would I do this as a volunteer?" If you can answer "yes" to that, then you're definitely in the right career.

THE IMPORTANCE OF PLANNING YOUR TIME

The first step in preparing to give great in-flight service is to understand the time factors. You learned in Chapter 8 that time must be deducted from the total ETE (estimated time en route) for the plane to climb to altitude, level off to cruising-speed and then later, descend to land. All your service activity then will be done during that cruising period.

You will also need to know an additional system of timing because many of your flights will involve traveling through different time zones that will indicate the type of service you provide at that cruising altitude. Your dual watch may say that it's dinner time back home, but when you collect your passengers, they're on breakfast time. They would think you rather odd if you started mixing drinks and pouring wine at seven o'clock in the morning! To avoid this you are now going to learn a new system of keeping time. Although it may seem confusing in the beginning, ultimately you will find that it avoids confusion because the time is universal and can be used worldwide.

THE 24-HOUR CLOCK

By using the 24-hour clock, each of the 24 hours in a day has been given a figure based on time in Greenwich, England, and is called the Universal Coordinated Time. By eliminating a.m. and p.m., this allows people to use a standard time no matter what part of the world's 28 time zones they are in.

The starting point for the 24-hour system begins with 0000 hour right after midnight, Greenwich time, and progresses through 2400 hours until midnight. Minutes are added on after the hour figure; for example, 11.45 p.m. becomes 2345. 11.45 a.m. becomes 1145.

24-HOUR CLOCK

```
 1.00 = 0100/1300
 2.00 = 0200/1400
 3.00 = 0300/1500
 4.00 = 0400/1600
 5.00 = 0500/1700
 6.00 = 0600/1800
 7.00 = 0700/1900
 8.00 = 0800/2000
 9.00 = 0900/2100
10.00 = 1000/2200
11.00 = 1100/2300
12.00 = 1200/2400
```

To further complicate matters there are also time zones. The world is divided into 28 time zones with one-hour difference between each adjoining zone. In the United States of America we have four major time zones.

Listed below are the time zones with their respective abbreviations and times measured in relation to Greenwich Mean Time (GMT). All times west of Greenwich are behind (-) and all times east of Greenwich are ahead (+). These are often referred to, for example, as Eastern Standard Time (EST), Central Standard Time (CST), Mountain Standard Time (MST) or Pacific Standard Time (PST).

Eastern	EST	-5
Central	CST	-6
Mountain	MST	-7
Pacific	PST	-8

Finally, you must take into account daylight savings where further changes must be made according to the season. In spring, add an hour and in the fall, deduct an hour; i.e., spring forward or fall back. Practice this a few times and it will become quite easy. If you still experience difficulty check with the pilots – they're seldom wrong. Somehow, they always seem to know how to get the plane to land right on time.

TAKING CARE OF THE PASSENGERS

Cabin service should be done quickly and quietly without interrupting the passengers, unless they ask. Do not give the appearance that you are listening to their conversations or watching them in their activities. You are there to serve only and not participate.

Once the Pilot-In-Command turns the seatbelt sign off everyone except yourself is urged to keep theirs on during the duration of the flight; however, most of the passengers know that being able to fly at an altitude of 40,000 feet and above usually renders a very calm flight, so be prepared to maneuver your way around a lot of mobile people.

PREPARING THE FOOD AND BEVERAGES

The most important aspect concerning your work in the galley is cleanliness. This means that your hands must be washed before and after touching food and gloves should be worn when preparing it. To protect your clothing, wear an apron, and if your hair is long, tie it back.

THE FIRST TASK

Your first task now is to pour glasses of bottled water, add a slice of lime or lemon to each and then proceed through the cabin, giving one to each passenger. Place beverage napkins down for the drinks and in case of turbulence, give them a lap napkin as well. Although some may refuse the water, advise them that they should drink at least one glass of water per hour to counteract the dehydrating effects of being in a pressurized cabin at high altitude. Replenish their water glasses at least once every hour and please, don't forget the pilots.

INTO THE GALLEY

Once you're back in the galley start brewing the coffee and while it is brewing, prepare any special drink orders and small snack trays. Cocktails and mixed drinks should be filled to the top of the glass; however, when pouring wine, only fill the glass to about two-thirds full so that they can swirl the wine around and smell the aroma if desired. When a passenger requests another cup of coffee, give them a new cup on a clean tray with new provisions each time. Coffee not only tastes better in a new cup, but combined with the new, clean tray, adds a nice touch to the quality of service.

If the meal you are serving is a boxed luncheon then you should have found a caterer who has made them all look exquisite. Some caterers go all out in the packaging and decorations so that it becomes hard to believe that it's food inside and not jewelry from Tiffany's! If this is what you have then you can serve the boxed luncheons straight to the table. Your passengers will love them! All you will need to do is give each person a place mat, silverware, napkins and, of course, a beverage.

Occasionally a boxed luncheon will look terrible although the food inside is delicious. If this is the case, remove the food from the box and arrange it decoratively on a plate. Be creative with the layout and add your own garnishments if necessary. Sculpture the vegetables and fruit where possible, or add a cluster of grapes, sprigs of parsley, some large strawberries with the tops on, and you will considerably enhance a dull-looking meal.

On special occasions such as birthdays present the cake but never light any candles. This is a dangerous practice in an aircraft and should never be considered because of the possibility of fire.

TABLE SERVICE ETIQUETTE

SETTING THE TABLE

When setting the table, make sure all patterned plates are facing the same way. When carrying silverware to the table, place them on a napkin covered tray to help reduce the noise. Never touch areas that will come into contact with their mouth or their food; for example, the prongs of a fork or the blade of a knife. Make sure you have color coordinated the place mats, napkins and napkin holders and that some sort of floral decoration is present. If the tables are full then you may want to place small, individual bouquets by each plate.

Although it's important to know the correct order in which to place silverware, it's advisable to put out just what's needed for each meal because of turbulence. The less you have out on a table the less chance of any mishaps.

SERVING THE WINE

When serving wine at the table pick up the glass by the stem and fill it away from those who are seated. You may also place a bottle of wine or champagne in an ice bucket so that they can serve themselves. Don't forget to place a napkin around the bottle to catch any moisture when the bottle is removed. It's also a good idea to place non-slip Velcro on the base of the ice bucket so that it won't slide when they use it.

A quick tip here is that when passengers are drinking wine always have a stack of towels close by to use in case of spillage.

SERVING THE FOOD

Before serving any food please ensure that you have removed your apron and gloves and that your outer clothing looks clean and presentable. I'm quite sure a food-or beverage-splattered flight attendant is not the image your company wants you to project.

When the time comes to serve the meal, make sure your fingers and thumbs are around the outer edges of the plates away from the food and that when you put the plates down, they are all facing the same way. If the meat is showing on the right side then place all the passengers' plates with the meat showing on the right side. Part of having an aesthetically appealing table setting is continuity in all that's visible.

Baskets of warm dinner rolls should be wrapped in a cotton napkin to retain the warmth and butter should be individually wrapped or singularly scooped and placed in a small container, to make it easier for the passengers and pilots to use. If sauces and gravies are left on the tables make sure they have a lid enclosure.

Remove the plates when everyone has finished and note what silverware is left for the next course, replacing any, if necessary. While the passengers are eating, keep an eye on what stage of the meal they are up to and if any drinks need to be refilled, especially the water. Make yourself available frequently in case they have a request for something additional while always being careful to maintain their privacy.

BACK IN THE GALLEY

While the passengers are eating, use this spare time to clean up the galley and prepare for the next course while being quiet in all you do. For items that need to be washed place them directly into a towel-lined or heavy-duty plastic container with a lid and secure tightly in the baggage compartment. This type of container is preferable to metal because it produces less noise and helps prevent breakage to the dishes.

TIME FOR AN INTERMEZZO?

You may want to add an intermezzo between the salad and the main course. This is common practice in upscale restaurants whereby they serve a small portion of citrus-flavored sorbet to cleanse the palate of any tastes from the previous course. This is an excellent idea if you are running behind time in preparing the main course; however; it does add up to a number of extra dishes and silverware, so make sure you still have enough left to serve the dessert.

CLEARING THE TABLE

Normally if you leave a table you place the napkin on the chair indicating you will be returning; however, in the cramped quarters of an aircraft don't adhere to such rules with your passengers. Napkins may be placed anywhere temporarily because of the limited space, so before you clear the table check first with everyone to ensure that they have indeed finished.

Just as you were careful to eliminate a lot of noise when you set the table, the same rule applies when you clear it. Using a towel-lined tray clear the table quickly and quietly, making sure that when you wipe the table you don't sweep crumbs into the passengers' laps.

The most important thing to remember in aircraft food service is that you are always in a moving environment. Turbulence is an ongoing factor and so everything you do must be done with that in mind. When you open food containers close them after each use and put them back from where they came before you start serving meals in the cabin. Everything should be stowed or stored away unless it's being used to improve safety.

TAKING CARE OF THE CREW

Without a doubt the pilots are the most important people in an airplane – once you've left the ground! You will probably agree that they need their strength and energy more than anyone else on the plane because they are the ones who have to make that precision landing at the end of the journey and get us all there safely. Surprisingly, many flight attendants neglect their meal service completely, especially when the cabin is full of passengers and the pace becomes hectic. This is wrong and quite dangerous.

To prevent this from ever happening – FEED THE PILOTS FIRST! As soon as the seatbelt sign is turned off, go to the cockpit, get their orders and then serve them. After the passengers have been served go back and see if there is anything else they require. Remember that it's difficult for them to leave the cockpit because of their workload and so you should be the one to visit them.

Special consideration should also be given to the preparation of their food. Remove food wrappings to make it easier for them to eat off a tray behind the yoke in a cramped cockpit. Extra precaution should be taken to ensure that beverages, sauces or other fluid items, cannot spill onto their flight equipment. Just because you are going to make it easier for them to eat, it doesn't mean you can make it less attractive. If you give them the same consideration in food presentation and garnishments you will go a long way in promoting good crew morale and continuity, not to mention keeping your job.

SPECIAL SERVICES

Occasionally you may be asked to cater for a religious or cultural group where different catering and food rules apply. The easiest way to fulfill these requests is to check the Yellow Pages of the telephone directory or contact the respective church, temple or cultural association in the area. In a kosher meal, for example, food must be served in separate dishes and a rabbi must personally bless everything according to Orthodox Jewish laws. Most caterers would not be able to meet this request so a call to a Jewish temple will probably result in a rabbi's coming to the plane and providing assistance to you.

Special and unusual requests are not that common, but be prepared to cater for them when they do. You will find that they are not only an interesting break from the usual routine, but enable you to learn a little more about the wonderful diversity of our humanity.

IN-FLIGHT EMERGENCIES

It is imperative that you fully understand what is required of you in an emergency situation because a plane flying at an altitude of 40,000 feet and above, will take some time to descend and land before help can arrive. Turbulence has been known to cause broken limbs and severe bleeding, and fearful flyers have been known to develop hyperventilation or even go into cardiac arrest. Strains of bacteria have caused chronic food poisoning and pregnant moms have gone into premature labor. Passengers have even choked on food requiring the flight attendant to administer the Heimlich manuever (abdominal thrust), until their blocked airway was cleared. If they had waited half an hour for the plane to land it would have been too late. While the Pilot-In-Command must be informed of any in-flight emergency, you will be the one expected to attend to the emergency situation.

When you render assistance, be aware that today we seem to have an abundance of blood-borne, air-borne and numerous natural diseases that make transmission easy unless you follow certain precautions. Always try to avoid contact with any bodily fluids, if possible, by using a clean towel or disposable gloves. This is even more important if you have an open wound such as a cut or scratch on an exposed area of your body. Be careful not to touch bloodstained clothing or any other objects that may be around them and do not touch any areas of your body, especially your nose, eyes, ears and mouth until you have been able to wash your hands thoroughly.

The greatest problem with in-flight emergencies is panic. If you are well prepared and know how to stay calm, assess the situation, and take immediate action, there will be less chaos. You will receive thorough instruction on in-flight emergencies when you go for your training and after this you are strongly encouraged to stay informed of the latest techniques and equipment available through aviation safety specialists.

PREPARING FOR ARRIVAL

Half an hour before the plane is to land it is a nice gesture to give everyone a moist wash towel with which to freshen up. When you enter the cockpit to give the pilots theirs, check with them for information on current weather and anything else at the destination that may be of interest to the passengers. At the same time, give them any information concerning passenger requests such as transportation or hotel changes. As you walk back through the cabin to collect the towels, collect all other items that need to be moved prior to landing and relay the pilot's information to them. Most will appreciate this information, especially if it's snowing at the destination and minus ten degrees! There will probably be some rummaging through the baggage compartment for "extra accessories."

DESCENT

Once the plane leaves the cruising altitude and begins the descent this is the time that you should complete the final stages of preparing the cabin interior for landing. This means you have only twenty minutes left.

COCKPIT
- Check with the pilots first for items to be removed so that they will not need to be disturbed again.

GALLEY
- Place dirty dishes and other items into sealed containers and secure them in the baggage compartment.
- Clean coffee pot and thermos.
- Prepare passenger/crew comfort packs, if necessary.
- Inventory all supplies and prepare for next leg or trip.
- Remove trash to baggage compartment.
- Lock or secure all doors and cupboards.

LAVATORY/BATHROOM
- Remove trash to baggage compartment.
- Inventory supplies.
- Close/secure all drawers, cabinets and doors.

CABIN
- Remove or secure all moveable objects.
- Ensure all drawers, cupboards are secure.
- Check that passengers seatbelts are on and headrests in up position.
- Check that animals are secure.

BAGGAGE COMPARTMENT
- Check that all baggage, sealed containers and trash are secure.
- Check that emergency exits are clear.

Once you have gone through your checklists, start from the rear of the plane and slowly walk through to the front, checking to see if you have missed anything. This is also a good time to recheck that children still have their seatbelts on and animals are still secure. At this time confirm with the passengers that they know where they will be staying and where the crew can be reached. Often there will be changes to the itinerary, weather problems and so on, so you must all be able to stay in contact. Finally, notify the Pilot-In-Command that the cabin is ready for landing.

THE APPROACH

The approach part of the flight is when the plane lines up with the airport in order to land and it is often the most turbulent because of cloud conditions and cross winds. By the time the plane enters the approach, everyone on board should be seated for the final landing and should stay seated until the plane comes to a halt and the seatbelt signs are turned off.

THE LANDING

After the seatbelt sign has been turned off proceed to the rear of the plane and retrieve the passengers' coats and accessories for them. When they notify you they are ready to leave, prepare to assist them down the stairs with their hand luggage, children, pets and whatever else they have, and help them into their vehicles if necessary. While they wait for their baggage, go back into the cabin and give it a quick check to make sure nothing was left behind. Because of turbulence that often accompanies the landing process, small items such as eyeglasses and books can fall behind cushions and seats. Always ask if the items left behind were meant to stay there for the next leg, otherwise you will probably be the one responsible for getting them to the passengers once the trip is over.

Finally, go to the baggage compartment and help pass out the baggage to the crew waiting below, whose members will place these into the passengers' waiting vehicles.

THE END OF THE JOURNEY

Once you come to the end of the journey make an effort to say goodbye to everyone who flew with you. Expect to be a little sad to see them go, especially if you have been traveling with them for a week or two. If it is appropriate, present each person with a small gift or token at this time. Some passengers give their flight crew lavish gifts, so be prepared for the surprise. If possible, share the gift with the rest of the crew; after all, they have worked just as hard as you and most of all, it's great for team spirit.

CLEAN-UP TIME

Once the passengers have departed your real cleaning work begins as you will need to prepare the plane's interior for the next journey so that all you will have to do then is take care of the catering.

CLEAN-UP CHECKLIST

- Tidy seats, pillows and blankets.
- Discard old newspapers and magazines.
- Brush or wipe ceiling and walls.
- Polish and clean all surfaces, including windows, bench tops and tables.
- Wash galley dishes and equipment.
- Clean bathroom/lavatory area.
- Inventory supplies in galley and bathroom.
- Clean out ice from refrigerator and drawer; towel dry.
- Refill water tanks.
- Make sure lavatory is serviced.
- Vacuum floors.
- Re-stock galley and bathroom with supplies you brought with you (or in hangar if at home base).
- Remove all trash.
- Give "Squawk's" List to Pilot-In-Command.

In very hot weather where temperatures exceed one hundred degrees Fahrenheit, pull the drapes or blinds and remove all food and medicines that may suffer heat damage. In very cold weather where temperatures go below the freezing point of thirty-two degrees Fahrenheit or lower, empty the water tanks and drain the toilet to prevent freezing and breaking of the pipes. Remove all bottles, cans (including sodas), or any other jars of liquid that may freeze and break as well. If baggage is left on the plane, check with everyone to ensure that nothing inside could break, also. Any items to be removed can usually be stored in an airport terminal (FBO) if necessary. Consult with the FBO employees.

PART FOUR: AFTER THE FLIGHT

CHAPTER 12: LIVING WITH THE CREW

GETTING ACQUAINTED

It's quite common for the Pilot-In-Command to be responsible for the hiring of the flight crew, including the flight attendant. After a tentative hiring decision is made it is also possible for the crew to take the prospective flight attendant out for a meal to get better acquainted; after all, they are probably going to be spending a lot more time with each other than they are with their families. If at anytime during this meeting you feel that the position is not going to fulfill your expectations, then don't accept the position, but look for one more suitable. The reason is simple. Flight crews often work long hours and suffer the consequences of jet lag, extreme weather conditions, poor lodging facilities in poverty-ridden, third-world countries, while remaining away from their home and families for long periods at a time. When you are away on trips they will be your "family" and you will get to spend a lot of time sharing the same lodgings, meals, transportation and so on. Obviously it makes sense to be working only with those whom you want to be around.

At first these constraints on your lifestyle may not appear too difficult because your job seems to be quite a novelty; however, as the weeks and months go by, you will find that it takes a special kind of person who can handle the physiological, psychological and interpersonal relationship stresses that result from this. At the end of the day in most jobs you leave the office and your coworkers, and go home to be with your family and friends. In corporate aviation however, you go "home" with your coworkers so the final decision you make will have a great impact not only on you but the rest of the crew you are going to be with.

ACCOMMODATION

Usually the company or the Pilot-In-Command makes prior arrangements for the crew's accommodations. Upon arrival at a hotel you may be expected to pay for your lodgings with a credit card so make sure you have one. As we discussed in Chapter six, Visa, MasterCard and American Express are widely accepted and to a lesser extent, the Discover Card. At the completion of each trip you will submit an expense report to the Pilot-In-Command, who will approve it and forward it to the company for reimbursement. Sometimes, companies will provide the crew with a company credit card, which makes it easier for you, but does not allow you to collect the hotel and airline points and rewards associated with them.

When you are assigned your room, make sure you have the room and/or telephone numbers of the crew, especially the Pilot-In-Command. You must know how to reach each other at any given time of the day in case of changes in schedule, emergencies (natural disasters, political unrest) and for meeting at meal times, if necessary. During your stopover, try to be in contact with one of them at least once a day so that someone knows of your activities in the event of schedule or other changes.

DINING OUT

Always maintain a professional image when you're away on a trip and that includes when you're off duty and in the crew's company. Remember that you're probably with the person who hired you or who helped make that decision and so they can just as easily fire you if you step beyond the company bounds. Avoid alcohol if possible, or if you must drink, do it with discretion. Any drunken episodes may be witnessed by more than your crew members, especially if it's the only hotel in town – your passengers could be there, too!

There will also be times when you will have to dine alone and you have one of two choices. You can order room service or you can go down to the dining room. If you choose the latter, take a book or magazine to read to discourage unwanted dinner partners. Stay away from the bar even if the waiter asks you to go there to wait until your table is ready. Instead, wait at the entrance to the dining room with everyone else. Remember, you're not on vacation and you're not at home – you're away on a business trip.

CONCIERGE LOUNGES

Some hotels have concierge lounges where for a few extra dollars you can stay on a designated floor designed for business and professional travelers and enjoy the services provided in total peace and comfort. You can converse with others if you wish, or simply take a book, read a newspaper, watch the television or catch up on business. Superb food and drinks are offered free of charge (except alcohol), in the mornings and evenings. There is also a concierge attendant, who will be able to assist you with any matters concerning your stay in the hotel or town. If your company allows it, this is definitely the way to travel.

PERSONAL SECURITY

Unfortunately, crime is everywhere and no one is exempt from becoming a victim. To reduce your chances of this happening observe the following:

- **HOTELS**: You will find their security information printed on cards or in brochures in your room. Sometimes they can be viewed on the in-house television station. If you are uncertain about anything regarding your safety, call the front desk and they will assist you immediately.

- Hotels usually advise:

  1. Never open the door to anyone unless you have called for them. Identify callers using the peephole.
  2. Report anything suspicious to the operator or security.
  3. Always lock your door and windows even in a skyscraper.
  4. Keep valuables in a safe place – or leave them in the locked safe.

- **PUBLIC TRANSPORT/PERSONAL SAFETY**: The Pilot-In-Command will normally arrange for a vehicle for the crew to use during their time of stay. This is standard procedure with most companies. You may, however, decide to do some exploring on your own. Observe the following guidelines carefully.

  1. Check with concierge/reception for tips on safety.
  2. Use the hotel guest transportation if possible.
  3. Preferably, take a crew member/friend with you.
  4. Take a map if you don't know the route.
  5. Observe the type of people around you – do you feel comfortable with them?
  6. Carry your hotel address and phone number with you.
  7. Carry a cell-phone and spare battery on you where you can reach it in a hurry.
  8. Don't look like a tourist/traveler.
  9. Carry a dummy wallet with you. Hide the valuable one on your person.
  10. Don't go into dark and unlit areas.

11. Tell the crew where you are going and how they can reach you.
12. Turn back if you have doubts.

When arriving into a new place spend some time with the aviation personnel in the terminal service center. They will be able to advise you on the best restaurants, hotels, places to see and most of all, places to stay away from. Sometimes the danger in some of these places is not from people but animals, such as bears and mountain lions. In isolated areas of Alaska and the Northern Rockies it can become dangerous walking back to your lodgings at night. The meal you just ate may become a predator's, too – so be careful.

Then there are the road conditions to be wary of. In places such as Montana, after the snow and ice have melted away, there are often huge holes left behind in the roads. The roads and streets outside of the main city area are not always lit and in poor visibility, they can be extremely dangerous. Once again, heed the advice from the locals and always let the crew know where you are going and when you are expected back.

WORKING AS A TEAM

The continued success of your team is dependent upon all of you working together in a professional manner although you are traveling together in a family/friend type of environment. Your jobs require peak performance, almost like that of a champion athlete, and how you perform on the outside is greatly affected by how you condition yourself on the inside. In other words, the quality of your life begins with you and greatly affects the lives of others.

Because of the uniqueness of your working environment I have listed a few tips that will help you in coping with this unusual type of working relationship.

- Do not criticize, condemn, or judge your crew members.
- If you can't say or do something positive or worthwhile – don't say or do it.
- Never yell or scream at them.
- Don't be afraid to admit you're wrong.
- Be honest in absolutely everything.
- Listen to them and encourage them to talk about themselves.
- Smile – be friendly!
- Use their name when communicating.
- Show tireless, positive energy in helping all members of your team.
- Don't flirt with the crew members.
- Never become intimate with them.
- Express your feelings in a positive and productive manner.
- Think of team spirit – not the "I" spirit.
- Develop and encourage the right attitude with everyone.
- Be flexible, teachable, amiable and caring.
- If you really hate your job, quit – so that someone else can enjoy it.

PART FIVE: INTERNATIONAL FLIGHTS

CHAPTER 13: INTERNATIONAL NECESSITIES

Unlike local trips, international flights require a new set of rules and regulations that need to be adhered to closely. Failure to observe them could result in illness, fines, denied entry into a country or even imprisonment. Remember, that when you are in a foreign country you are visiting as a guest. As a flight attendant you will play a vital role in contributing to the success of these overseas journeys. Often you will be interacting with consulates and embassies for passports and visas, and assisting passengers in all stages of the journey, covering everything from health requirements to safety and security, as well as providing first-class service on board. It's on these international journeys that your leadership and organizational skills will truly be realized.

CULTURAL DIFFERENCES

Perhaps the most exciting aspect of international travel is the cultural differences that exist and it is these differences that makes our world so special. International travel is probably going to make up a good part of your career and so realizing that people are representatives of the environment that has nurtured them will go a long way to making your journeys a success.

In Saudi Arabia, for example, women are very restricted in many areas of their lives compared to the men. They must wear a long black gown called a "chador" that covers them from head to foot when in public. They are not allowed to drive a car, shop without a male chaperone, and they must walk behind their husband – never beside him in public. In restaurants, male and females are separated into different areas; however, if you can prove you are married by showing a marriage license, you can dine together in the family room. This may irritate many westerners who are used to a completely different lifestyle, but when you're in a foreign land, obey the rules and if that poses a problem then don't become a flight attendant, because the rest of the team won't be able to depend on you.

A tourist can choose where they want to travel; however, as a flight attendant you go where the company sends you. This may mean camping out in the Amazon jungle with a team of photographers, or backpacking over the Himalayas with the boss additional to your cabin work. Some flight attendants have left the duties of the cabin upon landing to become a nanny to the boss's children while sailing around the Mediterranean on a huge yacht. Each international journey can involve many cultures and contrasting lifestyles, so be prepared for an incredible change of pace.

LEGALITIES

In preparing for international travel a number of legal requirements must be completed before a journey can begin. In this section the following will be covered:

- Passports, visas and visa agencies
- Customs and immigration, crew and passenger manifest, general declarations
- Health requirements, immunizations

PASSPORTS, VISAS AND VISA AGENCIES

Once you receive notification that an international journey is planned you must first look at the trip sheet to determine where you will be traveling to during each of the legs, and who the passengers will be. You will then need to obtain from the passengers (as well as all the crew), passport information and advise them to get any visas and immunizations if required. Visa and immunization information can be obtained in a number of ways:

- Consulates and embassies
- Travel agents
- Visa service companies

The best source for updated information on all consulates and embassies is the "Diplomatic List" published by the Department of State Publication, Office of the Chief of Protocol. This can be purchased at:

Superintendent of Documents
U.S. Government Printing Office
Washington, D.C. 20402,
U.S.A.

Travel agents are also a good source for information, along with the airlines. If your company does a lot of international flying, or goes to countries not frequented by many crowds of tourists, then you may want to obtain the services of a visa service company. Generally, they will arrange for business and tourist visas, for passports – U.S. and non-U.S. passports; visa photos, as well as applicable information on the requirements and restrictions concerning the countries you wish to visit. Once you have established an account with them you will find the process of taking care of the legal necessities a lot easier. Make sure when you get passport information from the passengers and crew, that you write them on your passenger profile lists for future reference. This will save bothering them again on future trips.

For information on visa service companies check through all the ones listed on the Internet or the Yellow Pages of your telephone book.

If you decide to get the information yourself then you should contact each of the consulates or embassies for the countries listed on your trip sheet and obtain the current entry requirements for all passengers and crew. This should be done each time a visit is required because political, security and health changes can happen overnight and what you can do one day, may be prohibited the next day.

Also, some passengers may be traveling with foreign passports, so it is imperative that they meet all the legal requirements necessary for their entry into the countries specified. Never assume that permission will be granted once you arrive. They have the right to deny any foreign aircraft containing passengers who have not met the entry requirements.

The U.S. State Department issues Consular Information Sheets, Travel Warnings and Public Announcements that are available for every country of the world. **Consular Information Sheets** inform Americans of the location of the nearest American Consulate or Embassy where they will be visiting, along with additional information on political disturbances, health problems, crime and security issues or anything else that is not critical enough to issue a Travel Warning. They are solely a fact sheet and leave the decision to travel to a country the responsibility of the person. A **Travel Warning**, however, advises all Americans to avoid certain countries for a length of time because of immediate danger, whereas a **Public Announcement** is issued for short-term problems such as terrorist threats against Americans.

If you are traveling with passengers holding foreign passports then you should advise them to check with their embassy or consulate for the same information. What may be safe for an American to visit may be dangerous for another nationality and vice versa. As a backup, you may want to check the security of the foreign passengers as well because you will all be traveling together and what might affect them could possibly affect you, too.

CUSTOMS AND IMMIGRATION

When you travel overseas you must remember that a foreign country's laws and regulations can be quite different from what you are used to and despite how senseless some of them may appear to be, they must be obeyed.

The Pilot-In-Command is ultimately responsible for ensuring that all passengers on board proceed directly to the customs and immigration area once they leave the plane. You will be vital in assisting the crew in coordinating the passengers to act in a responsible manner. When requested by the customs officials everything must be taken off the plane for inspection and in some cases, this may even include the trash for them to search through. Don't argue - just do as they say, because they have the power while you're in their territory.

Each passenger, including children and the crew, is required to complete an **Immigration Card.** Once approved this will be the permit allowing everyone to stay in that country. It must be kept on you at all times (preferably with your passport) and surrendered to the airport authorities when you leave the country. If a stay is extended then these cards will need to be re-approved by an immigration officer at the nearest airport.

Reentry into the United States will also require proof of citizenship or residency. Always check that anyone who is an alien resident has an Alien Registration Card (Form I-551) as well.

The Pilot-In-Command of the aircraft must present to customs and immigration in each country a **General Declaration,** that you will probably write - often in multiple copies, that details pertinent information about the plane and its passengers. A good tip with these is to keep some carbon paper on board to make all the duplicates. Proof of citizenship is required for each person and this can be in the form of a passport, birth certificate or a naturalization document; however, a passport is the preferred and often the only acceptable means of entry into the majority of countries.

There will also be a **Customs Declaration** form to fill out in which passengers' state any dutiable goods they have that need to be declared for tax purposes. Advise your passengers not to lie or conceal any dutiable goods because if they are found, they will likely pay a hefty penalty which is often far more than the price of the actual goods, or even worse, the goods may be confiscated. Honesty is definitely the best policy.

Please advise your passengers well in advance of the items that are prohibited unless special permission is received from pertinent sources; for example, a doctor taking medications to a hospital in Somalia or spear fishing equipment going to a diving group in Fiji. Of course these must be declared, or proper documentation shown (preferably with the approval from the host country's embassy) to any customs official who asks. Firearms, drugs, and live plants and fish are generally prohibited from entry in most places. In the case of firearms and drugs, arrest and imprisonment are almost certain and in some cases planes are confiscated as well, leaving the rest of the crew and passengers to find their way home by some other means. Prohibited goods are a serious issue so make sure everyone completely understands the consequences if they fail to observe them.

Most countries also allow adults entering their boundaries to bring in a certain amount of **duty-free goods,** such as alcohol and tobacco. This information can be obtained when you initially plan for the journey. Where possible, obtain printed information on this and hand one to each passenger for their reference. Before you land ask them if they have read it and understand what the requirements are.

Pets and other animals require special permits to enter most countries. Sometimes it's just having proof of a current rabies certificate; however, never travel to a country without having first investigated and obtained all the papers required for entry. Usually a pet owner will have to obtain a U.S. Customs Shipper's Export Declaration, a rabies vaccination certificate and a veterinary health certificate and all these can be obtained from international air carriers. Some countries also have automatic quarantine periods that can last for several months for some pets. Others such as the United Kingdom are starting to change their quarantine rules for admitting pets. The only way to be completely safe is to check with the consulate or embassy of the country you intend to visit. Also, check what the requirements are for bringing the pet back into the USA. Failing to observe any of the above could result in the animal's being quarantined for many months, confiscated, or your aircraft being denied entry into the country.

It's also important to be aware of the fact that what we may enjoy and keep as pets in this country can be a food delicacy in others. Cats and dogs, for example, are highly prized menu items in Vietnam, China and Mongolia and the chances are that if any animals are confiscated there, it may be the last time you see them. Make sure your passengers have wisely considered all the issues before traveling with their pets.

SAMPLE GENERAL DECLARATION
(Agriculture, Customs, Immigration, and Public Health)

FROM: Macapa, Brazil   TO: Acapulco, Mexico

OPERATOR: Johnson Corp.
AIRCRAFT MODEL: G-11   REGISTRATION: N1234Y   DATE: 15 Jan, 1999

CREW MANIFEST

LAST & FIRST NAME	FUNCTION	NATIONALITY	PASSPORT #
Woods, John	Captain	USA	B123456
Morgan, Peter	F/O	USA	B654321
Williams, Jane	F/Engineer	U.K.	E12346
Stubbs, Amber	F/Attendant	USA	B67854311

PASSENGER MANIFEST

LAST & FIRST NAME	PASSPORT #	NATIONALITY	DATE OF BIRTH
Sinclair, Barry	05678916	USA	December 12, 1953
Sinclair, Mary	04657827	USA	January 1, 1958
Sinclair, William	59687828	USA	July 10, 1982
Sinclair, Kathie	67854329	USA	October 15, 1987
Heikle, Katerina	UZ05231	Germany	August 12, 1970
Jorgansen, Frederike	SY655Z1	Austria	January 9, 1972
Obed, Nathalia	JYZX564	Israel	November 11, 1981

DECLARATION OF HEALTH

Illness, viruses, plants, animals present?

NONE

_____

I declare that all statements contained in this General Declaration are true and correct:

SIGNATURE _____
        Authorized Agent or Pilot-In-Command

HEALTH REQUIREMENTS/IMMUNIZATIONS

Immunization requirements for some countries are subject to change, often with little or no advance warning. These changes can also affect reentry into the Unites States as well. To ensure that you and your passengers are protected from diseases prevalent in some of these places, you should check with the consulate or embassy when you request travel information. The World Health Organization requires that its members notify them regularly of the immunization requirements for entry into their countries.

In the United States, many immunizations are given in childhood; however, some people migrate here without having had to meet this requirement. It is essential, therefore, that any passengers who have not had protection from these childhood diseases, check with the U.S. Public Health Service or their local government health agency first, before traveling into areas that may cause a problem.

If passengers or crew travel without having the appropriate health certificates, then some countries may place the person in isolation for surveillance. This may also occur if you have the necessary papers but have arrived from endemic or infected areas; for example, from Africa during an ebola or cholera outbreak. Sometimes a country may specify that immunizations against typhoid, cholera, yellow fever and so on are not necessary, but it may be wise to go ahead and get immunized for your own protection, especially if traveling to third-world countries where sickness and disease are prevalent.

Anyone requiring immunization should do so well in advance as certain types such as smallpox and yellow fever require a two-week separation between them. There should also be time available for the person to recuperate from any reaction to the immunization.

If a passenger or fellow crew member becomes sick do not administer medicines or drugs, but do provide first aid and summon professional help as quickly as possible. Medical help can be obtained in most places around the world; however, there are always some exceptions. Once again the American consulate or embassy personnel will be able to advise you of the closest English-speaking physician in your area. The American military, is located throughout the world also and can often assist. Most hotels, however, can usually summon an English-speaking physician when requested. If a person dies, you should notify the Pilot-In-Command first, then the local police, the American Embassy and their next-of-kin immediately.

AMERICAN CONSULATES AND EMBASSIES ABROAD

The American consulates and embassies abroad are involved in numerous diplomatic concerns as well as being available to assist Americans during times of severe difficulties while they are in foreign lands. Assistance would be given in times of arrest and/or imprisonment, missing passports and visas, violence or bodily harm, natural disasters, political unrest, terrorist activity, becoming stranded or destitute, and illness, injury or death.

Minor problems that can be handled by crew members, the hotel manager or local officials are not their concern. They are there to provide emergency assistance only and cannot act as lawyers, judges, bankers or doctors. While they may render certain legal aid, the passengers and crew must be aware that everyone comes under the laws of the land that they are in. You could be executed in Saudia Arabia for adultery, publicly whipped in Singapore for theft, or sentenced to life imprisonment in Thailand for drug possession. The consulate or embassy officials would notify those back home that your needs are extremely urgent and advise you of what has been done to protect your rights as an American citizen. They cannot, however, go beyond those limits.

MISCELLANEOUS

In addition, a number of other important factors contribute to the success of an international journey. These include:

- Water
- Food
- Hotel accommodations
- Currency, credit cards, tips and gratuities
- Communication

WATER

If you always assume that the drinking water outside of America is contaminated, then the chances of your getting sick are greatly reduced. Although water may be chlorinated and is quite palatable to the local inhabitants, it may not be safe for you. Bacteria such as E. coli or Giardia lamblia, a protozoan, can still contaminate chlorinated water and, consequently, may give you a serious bowel infection, along with vomiting and painful diarrhea. If you decide to use the local water, boil it for at least fifteen minutes first to kill any bacteria present.

Drink bottled water where possible, especially if boiling it is not an option. When ordering bottled water, check the label to see where it is produced. If it's local then the risks are probably still the same. If bottled water which you know to be safe is not available, such as Evian from France, then request a sparkling water such as Perrier from France or Pellegrino from Italy, or a club soda. Companies such as Coco-Cola and Pepsi, for example, export canned and bottled drinks worldwide and usually guarantee a safe source of drinkable products.

The water you use for drinking or brushing your teeth should be from bottled water and unless you know for sure that ice cubes have been made from it or that food items such as tomatoes or celery have been washed in it, don't touch them. In a restaurant, always ask the waiter to bring the bottle to the table and then open and pour it so you can see that what you are drinking is indeed from that bottle. Never drink from the bottle as the exterior may have been exposed to contaminates. Always use a glass or a clean, pre-wrapped straw.

Bathing and showering poses another problem. Before you bathe or shower, turn on the taps and let the water run for a while. This will not only help clear the pipes leading into your tub and provide cleaner water, but will also wash away any residue left behind in the tub. In some places you may have to disinfect the washing area before you get in. In conditions like this always wear protection for your feet. The important point to remember here is to avoid swallowing any water, or letting it get into your eyes, ears, nose or any sores or wounds on your body. Dirty, contaminated water getting onto an insect bite or a shaving cut, can result in serious infections later, so don't take risks. Towel wash yourself with bottled water if the conditions are really bad. Also, avoid swimming pools and spas in suspect areas as well.

A key point to remember is that the water tanks on your aircraft cannot be refilled in many countries. This means you will have to take lots of large bottles of water to use when the water tanks are empty. When ice is obtained for storing foods, place the ice in sealed plastic bags to prevent the melting water from touching any of the food or beverage products.

A good way to check on food and beverage conditions in some of these places is to check with the airlines because they usually have their own caterers and are generally known to be safe worldwide. They may, upon request, agree to service your aircraft, too.

FOOD

DAIRY PRODUCTS

Dairy foods such as milk, cheese, raw eggs, yogurt, ice cream, butter, custards, mayonnaise, whipped cream and regular creams should be avoided even if the containers say they are pasteurized. Many of the pasteurized products produced by some countries would never pass the stringent health regulations required in the United States. If necessary, make your own milk up by using powdered or evaporated milk and mixing it with bottled water.

MEAT, SEAFOOD AND POULTRY

All meat, seafood and poultry should be well cooked. Avoid eating any type of raw shellfish such as oysters, along with steak tartare (raw ground beef) and sushi (raw fish) – unless you're in a first-class environment. Even then the risks are yours. Check before you leave home that the countries you will be visiting have not had recent outbreaks of Mad Cow disease or any other communicable disease. Even sophisticated places such as the United Kingdom and Argentina have had recurring problems, so it's diner beware!

FRUIT AND VEGETABLES

These should be washed with bottled water or cooked at a high temperature to kill bacteria. Choose fruits that have thick skins and can be peeled without having to wash them. Also avoid all uncooked or buffet-style food that may have been sitting in the display for a long time as these are great environments for producing bacteria.

The golden rule when it comes to eating, drinking, or buying catering anywhere overseas, is never to buy it from street vendors or outdoor restaurants. Food and beverages in these places cannot be adequately stored or cooked properly and are constantly exposed to all the elements such as dust and pollution, along with bugs and insects.

HOTEL ACCOMMODATIONS

Usually the company or the Pilot-In-Command or company personnel will take care of the international accommodations for the crew. If you are expected to do this then make sure that you check with the respective embassy or consulate first before making any bookings in unknown destinations. Check also with the airlines and travel companies for additional information, if necessary.

In most parts of the world it's usually the most expensive hotel that is the best and safest because of all the security. Even the poorest places in the world seem to have a "first-class" place to stay and if you do choose to stay in one, just remember to check what goes with the price. The bed may be an optional extra!

Additionally, if you are the one responsible for taking the baggage to the individual rooms, you may also want to check that there is an elevator, and a bellboy to assist you in the delivery. Make sure you tip the bellboy generously; otherwise, he may not be there on a return visit.

Not every hotel or place of accommodation can afford to give you high quality bedding and in some places it seems, cannot afford to wash the linens after use. If space is available you may want to pack your own lightweight sleeping bag or take along some personal antiseptic or bug spray while covering as much of your body as possible. Unfortunately, you may be able to travel first class, but you won't always be able to stay first class, but that's what makes the journeys so uniquely special. Of course, there's the opposite end of the spectrum where sumptuous indulgence of every kind is offered, so be sure to make the most of those opportunities for luxury when they come along.

CURRENCY, CREDIT CARDS, TIPS AND GRATUITIES

CREDIT CARDS

In most countries, personal checks are not accepted, so you should ensure that you have one of the major credit cards recognized around the world. Some countries request cash only as payment for services at airports and terminals and as a result, large amounts must be carried. When this happens leave the bulk of the money hidden in the plane and carry only what is needed for the land portion of the trip. Traveler's checks are good, but you will find as a flight attendant traveling frequently overseas, the time invested in obtaining them is not worthwhile. If you are unsure of the conversion rate use an international money converter available from many travel and office supply stores.

Many banks worldwide will now let you access your local bank with your ATM card. You may want to check the exchange rate and applicable fees before you make a withdrawal. Not only will you pay fees at the bank from which you withdrew money, but in some cases, your local bank will charge fees for the privilege of having international access, and these charges soon add up.

At most large airport terminals there are foreign exchange counters where you can exchange your money for local currency. Take into consideration when visiting places such as Europe, for example, where you could be going to multiple countries in a week. To avoid time delays, exchange your money into the currencies of all the places you will be going to all at once. Just remember, that other countries around the world enjoy public and national holidays, too, so you may want to check on that with the places you will be visiting so that you will have access to facilities once you arrive. In most cases the handler assigned to your aircraft will be able to assist you in circumstances such as these.

When making purchases of goods, refuse the salesperson's suggestion to ship the goods home, as often they will never arrive. The rule here is, if you can't carry the goods back to the plane, don't buy them.

Tipping is not always required overseas but where possible, try to do so unless it's really discouraged. Many establishments include the service tip in the bill, but often the service people never get to see that money. In some of the poorer countries, the service tip is all that separates them from a meal and starvation. Generously give for great service when you can and give to all those that help you. Not only are you helping those genuinely in need, but you're also guaranteeing great service upon your return.

COMMUNICATION

Once you have been assigned your room and notified the crew of your location and telephone number, contact the hotel operator for information on how to reach your office and family back home. Dialing out in some countries is extremely difficult and can be very expensive such as in Mexico, where it costs around $10.00 a minute. Sometimes communicating with an operator who does not speak English complicates the matter. A number of flight crew personnel have purchased cellular phones with worldwide access. This service may be expensive, but at least you know you can phone home with a minimum of fuss.

The Internet is another means of communicating around the world; however, some Muslim countries do not allow access due to religious and cultural laws. It's best not to rely on this as a universal means of communications. Ham radio, of course, is another great way to communicate, especially with the new portable models available on the market. All it takes is a license before you operate them.

In most countries the CNN news network is a great asset to travelers by providing current information on events around the world, along with updated weather and storm information. Some foreign hotels provide a newspaper written in English and of course, if you have access to the Internet, you have the latest information right at your fingertips.

CHAPTER 14: CATERING IN A FOREIGN LANGUAGE

Many countries are similar to the USA in that high quality food is always available along with reliable service to the aircraft. Unfortunately, there are a large number of places around the world where conditions are so poor or terrible that you have to take everything from home base. In these situations I cannot emphasize the importance of planning and coordinating everything so that your meal times away will be more enticing that a weekend camp-out and that there will still be room left in the baggage compartment for everyone's baggage.

HOW TO ORDER IN A FOREIGN LANGUAGE

I'm sure most corporate flight attendants will agree that international catering is quite a challenge when language is a barrier; in fact, because this is such a problem, some companies only hire flight crew who are bilingual. If you're interested in learning a language and are wondering which one to take then the best advice is to start learning the language of the country you will be visiting the most. The few words you learn will certainly go a long way toward making each journey there a more pleasant experience. In the meantime here's one great tip:

THE PICTURE BOOK

Trying to describe a three-course gourmet meal to a person when there is a language barrier is an exercise in futility. Often they say they know, but what you get is far removed from your original request. There is only one way to overcome this problem when you're not able to communicate and that is with pictures. A picture does say a thousand words and a picture album can save you hours of frustration and misery. Start preparing now and you will be very thankful later. There are a variety of ways to collect these:

- Ask caterers to send you pictures of their menus or take the photos yourself.
- Cut out pictures from magazines, newspapers, recipe books, and advertisements.
- Restaurant advertisements.
- Internet advertisements.
- Call food suppliers directly for pictures.

Once you have selected the pictures try to get numerous copies so that you have one for your file and one to give to the prospective caterer. If you have only one copy, then get extra color copies taken at an office supply store. Remember, when you travel you may have to give numerous copies of the same meal out over and over again, especially if it's an appetizer such as cheese and crackers, vegetable crudite – or the boss's favorite.

Place the original and the spare photo copies into individual plastic covers of a binder, separating them by the classification of the meal; for example – breakfast, lunch, dinner, appetizer, etc. You may want to add some paper to draw on as well. Once you encounter a language barrier with a caterer then simply pull out a picture for them to see. Use the spare paper to draw cutting, or serving techniques and once you're convinced they understand, let them keep a copy to assist them or their workers in making up your request. If this is one of your regular stopovers then get the caterer to write what they call it in their language. Write this name onto their copy and yours as well and the next time you call, ask for it by the name they gave you. Over time, you and the foreign caterer should both become familiar with your catering requirements and be experiencing a good working relationship.

WHAT SUPPLIES TO TAKE WITH YOU

The type of supplies you take will depend on the countries and the time or season of the year that you visit. If the journey requires a number of legs in various locations, then you will have to take additional supplies. The following will help you decide what to take and how to pack it on the plane so that the extra supplies won't make your galley look like an overstuffed supermarket.

When planning this refer to the extensive Aircraft Supplies List in Chapter 7, being careful to observe the following:

SOME DO'S AND DON'TS IN PLANNING YOUR PACKING LIST

- **Avoid all glass** such as bottles, jars and containers, that can break or explode in freezing temperatures.
- Buy **ready-made** varieties and avoid those that require adding water, if possible.
- All goods must be able to be **stored at room temperature** as refrigeration will be scarce.
- Buy **small packages** of everything because, once opened, food cannot be stored.
- Buy **multiple packs** of small goods.
- Look for healthful brands such as low salt/sodium, cholesterol and fat.
- **Fresh foods** such as meat, produce and dairy products cannot be taken into foreign countries.
- Canned seafood such as red salmon, tuna, sardines, anchovies, caviar have multiple uses.
- Make salads out of canned salad vegetables such as hearts of palm, bean medley, artichoke hearts.
- Look for **substitutes** such as Bacon Bits for bacon or Eggbeaters for eggs.
- Buy a lot of assorted **cereals** as they also make popular snacks.
- **Bread** can be brought "ready to cook" if it does not require refrigeration beforehand.
- **Dried fruits** such as prunes, apricots, dates, raisins can be used at almost any meal and add color.
- **Condiments** – buy assorted small packets only.
- Buy lots of **snack foods** such as chips and pretzels, plus crackers and pate.
- **Juices/milk** should be in cans or packages that do NOT require refrigeration.
- **Coffee** – buy small cans or individual packets.
- **Tea** – buy small individual packets only.
- Don't forget the **wine/beer** – some places don't have any.
- Take **ample paper goods** – also plates, cutlery, hot and cold beverage containers.
- Take large amounts of **assorted napkins**.
- Use **disposable dishes** for cooking in the microwave or oven.
- Stock up on **cleaning** supplies and **trash bags.**
- Buy additional **medicines** according to the country being visited.
- Use packaged **face/hand cleansing towels** instead of linen.
- Take ample **toilet rolls/hand soaps** – they're also in short supply worldwide.
- Take **sewing/shoe repair** kits.
- Take enough **bedding** for each seat on the plane, plus spares.
- Allow for a **week extra of food** to keep as spares.
- Substitute all **linen** for disposable equivalents where possible.
- **Picture books** of your country make nice gifts.
- **BOTTLED WATER – as much as the plane can carry!** Get assorted sizes.

As you go down the aircraft supplies list try to remember that you need to eliminate glass, fresh products after you leave the USA, goods that need refrigeration and anything that needs to be cleaned with water. In the galley, remove all surplus china, dishes and linens, to make way for disposable ones.

Depending on the length of the journey, you will need to pack in multiples of everything utilizing every ounce of space, so that you can still work efficiently.

GETTING ORGANIZED

Once you have determined the type and amount of food and beverages to take, examine the trip sheet and look at the following, still assuming that you are going to be doing the entire catering. A quick tip here is to write down sample meals for each leg and then make sure you have all the supplies. Rehearse these meals in your mind so that when the time comes you will feel more confident.

You will need to know:

- The total time away
- Number of legs which require meals
- The number of meals to be served within each leg – including snacks
- The type of country, environment
- The type of meal (gourmet/camping-out, lunch/dinner)
- The amount of time to serve the meals
- The total number of passengers and crew, plus extras
- The possible times your plane will be the "restaurant" for outside guests
- The type of weather expected for each meal; i.e., tropical or freezing

The amount of supplies you will require are obviously not going to fit within your tiny galley. To overcome this you will use sturdy ice chests that can easily be stored in the baggage compartment. Pack food items together according to the meals they will be used for:

Ice chest #1 – Appetizers, snack foods, condiments

Ice chest #2 – Canned/packet goods such as meat, seafood and soups

Ice chest #3 – Breakfast and lunch supplies

Ice chest #4 – Dinner supplies, dessert

The advantages of using ice chests is that they are cheap to buy and can be thrown out afterward if space is at a premium. They are also waterproof, light to carry, can double up as refrigeration containers, or they can be stacked neatly one inside of the other and used again for something else later on in the journey.

Items such as wine and beverages, toilet rolls, paper goods, etc., are too big and bulky to be placed into chests. Instead place these beside the stacked ice chests in an area of the baggage compartment where they will be easy to get at and have less chance of being damaged by anything else. Baggage and equipment will be loaded and unloaded numerous times throughout the journey so keep them away from the high traffic area. After the passengers and their baggage have left at the end of each leg, you can use this time to move about freely, restocking the supplies from what was stashed in the back of the baggage compartment. Make sure that your ice chests are marked on all sides as well as the top in large print so that the contents will be easily identifiable.

Additionally, carry enough strong-handled disposable bags (supermarket type) so as to make up care packages for the passengers and crew, if necessary. After a while you will get to know what each place is lacking and be able to make up a care package accordingly. Even if they don't want or don't need a package they nearly always want bottled water. Incidentally, I can't recall one passenger complaining because I gave them too much – most were exceedingly grateful that I had prepared for them just what they needed without ever having to ask.

CARE PACKAGES

It is already assumed that the passengers would have taken enough personal provisions for the stopover; however, many inexperienced travelers are not aware of how scarce various provisions can be in some countries. For this reason, and for the fact that it would be unnecessary to carry some of the supplies on each leg of the trip, you can prepare them if needed at each leg. Adjust the packages according to the weather, season and individual's tastes as per their personal profile list.

SAMPLE CARE PACKAGE

(2 NIGHTS STAY IN AMAZONIAN TERRITORY)

ACCOMMODATION FACTS: Water not drinkable, no bathroom accessories, cleanliness medium-low. **FOOD:** No breakfast and little/poor lunch facilities; great evening dinner at only restaurant in town.

> 4-6 small bottles each shampoo and conditioner
> 1 medium bath soap
> 1-2 large tissue packs
> Small personal bug spray/room spray/shower disinfectant
> Canned goods with pop-up tops/crackers
> Bag assorted nuts/licorice/trail mix
> 2-4 candy bars/Power Bars
> Dried fruit
> 4-6 liters water
> 2-4 cans soda/vegetable/fruit juice

MAKING MEALS FROM PACKAGED FOOD

Dining out on canned and packaged goods is a dreary thought even at the best of times, but it doesn't have to be that way. It is difficult though to make meals look and taste appetizing, so I would urge you to seek professional advice from a caterer or outdoor expert before you go. This will take a lot of the burden off you and with their experience to guide you, it will help to make it a lot more appetizing for the diners.

NOTE: In "camping out" like this, greater attention should be given to the decoration and presentation.

"CAMPING-OUT" PERSONAL PROFILE LIST

When planning the trip for your passengers take into account what their personal preferences are in canned and packaged goods by asking them to complete the following form. Remember that although they may love fresh corn, the thought of eating canned corned may be repulsive to them. Also, check whether they prefer the creamed, whole, diced or seasoned varieties. There are a lot of choices and I'm expecting that you will take the right choices with you when you go away.

The following can be used as a guideline in preparing your catering. Personalize it to meet the needs of your company, passengers and crew.

"CAMPING OUT" PERSONAL PROFILE LIST

CANNED/PACKAGED GOODS:
(Please write preference and specify whether creamed, whole, seasoned, salt-free etc.)

SNACKS:_____

APPETIZERS:_____

BREAKFAST ITEMS:_____

LUNCH ITEMS:_____

VEGETABLES:_____

MEATS: _____

POULTRY:_____

SEAFOOD:_____

DESSERTS:_____

BEVERAGES:_____

ADDITIONAL:_____

SAMPLES OF "CAMPING OUT" MENUS

BREAKFAST

Choice of the following:

OMELETS -Spanish/vegetable omelete – (using Eggbeaters), add canned mushrooms, onions, tomatoes; seasonings
BELGIUM WAFFLES (microwaveable) with pure maple syrup
ASSORTED CEREALS with raisins or prunes, boxed milk

WITH

Juices – canned or packaged
Tea/coffee

LUNCH OR DINNER

SOUP with breadsticks and crackers

and choice of:

HAM STEAK HAWAIIAN – canned ham with sliced canned pineapple, Minute Rice/potatoes
MEXICAN BEAN/BEEF TACOS with black olives, canned tomatoes, canned guacamole, chips and salsa
RED SALMON (canned Alaskan) with Minute Rice, canned corn, black olives
TUNA SALAD with rye or wheat crackers, dill pickles and olives
BEEF STEW (canned) with added vegetables including potatoes. Serve with crackers

AND

Packaged, canned assorted DESSERTS sprinkled and decorated with bottled maraschino cherries, nuts, chocolate sauce and instant custard mixes (made from powdered milk), etc.

NOTE: Decorate trays or tables with fresh flowers (silk flowers will do), if available, or plates with palm leaves if serving Ham Steak Hawaiian, for example, and fold paper napkins into decorative styles to enhance the look of the "cuisine." You and your passengers can have a lot of fun with bland food if you learn how to be a little more creative. Bon appetit!

PART SIX: CONCLUSION

CHAPTER 15: FINAL THOUGHTS

Eventually, there will come a time when I hope, after a long and rewarding career as a corporate flight attendant, it will be time to say goodbye and move on. Often circumstances such as family transfers, personal responsibilities or burn-out can be the reason, or perhaps it's just time to move on to another company or maybe even retire. When the time does come you will need to consider the following so that your departure will not cause conflict or an unnecessary burden to those you're leaving behind. To make the transition easier, try to observe the following:

- Once the decision has been made to leave notify your boss as soon as possible. Finding a replacement flight attendant who is familiar, or can be trained quickly, takes time and is greatly compounded by the fact that the flight crew is away on trips a lot of the time.

- When handing in your resignation (I hope it will be on good terms), sincerely express your thanks for the opportunity of working with the company, crew and all the passengers.

- Leave a contact number and address where you can be reached.

- Notify your customers, especially the caterers, of your decision to move on. No matter what the reason, speak positively about the company and people you're leaving, or don't say anything at all. Inform them of whom they can contact as your replacement. Remember, your business probably brought them a lot of income so be fair in your dealings with them; after all, it was your decision to leave that has affected them.

- Return all property to the company. Even if you bought that trinket for catering in Ethiopia, if it was bought out of the company money, it's theirs.

- Plan to restock everything before you depart and notify the companies from whom you made your purchases that a new person will be taking your job so that they can be ready to assist if needed. You may also suggest that they call in after you have left to introduce themselves to the new flight attendant. A thank-you card to them in the mail for services rendered is also a nice gesture.

- Notify all professional affiliations, if necessary.

- Speak with your attorney or accountant regarding the separation agreement with the company, if necessary.

- Remember your former company and coworkers with a card or note from time to time.

- Be prepared to share your knowledge and help others to achieve the same goals as you.

If you are planning on moving to a new company then I strongly advise you to do all of the above. Many times a flight attendant has transferred to a new company thinking that they will only be flying the owner around. Little did they know that the company decided to put their plane out on charter and guess who they ended up flying with again? Yes, you guessed right – their old boss! Always leave as professionally as possible, no matter how you may feel. Be thankful for the opportunity and experiences that you had, whether good or bad, while working with the former company. It's these experiences that later on you will treasure.

ADDENDA

During your training you will no doubt learn a lot of aviation terms that will benefit you in your work. One of the most useful terms is the phonetic alphabet which was created by the International Civil Aviation Organization (ICAO) as an international language for pilots. Using words instead of letters the phonetic alphabet helps to minimize confusion when communicating with anyone overseas.

THE PHONETIC ALPHABET

A	Alfa	(Al-fah)
B	Bravo	(Brah-voh)
C	Charlie	(Char-lee)
D	Delta	(Dell-tah)
E	Echo	(Eck-o)
F	Foxtrot	(Fox-trot)
G	Golf	(Golf)
H	Hotel	(Ho-tel)
I	India	(In-dee-ah)
J	Juliett	(Jew-le-ett)
K	Kilo	(Key-lo)
L	Lima	(lee-ma)
M	Mike	(Mike)
N	November	(No-vem-br)
O	Oscar	(Oss-car
P	Papa	(Pah-pah)
Q	Quebec	(Kwe-beck)
R	Romeo	(Row-me-oh)
S	Sierra	(See-air-rah)
T	Tango	(Tang-oh)
U	Uniform	(You-ne-form)
V	Victor	(Vic-tor)
W	Whiskey	(Wiss-key)
X	X-ray	(Ex-ray)
Y	Yankee	(Yang-kee)
Z	Zulu	(Zoo-loo)

NUMBERS

Numbers are spoken the same way with the exception of nine, which is spoken as "niner" so as distinguish it from the German word "nein" which means "no."

1	One	(Wun)
2	Two	(Two)
3	Three	(Three)
4	Four	(Fower)
5	Five	(Fife)
6	Six	(Six)
7	Seven	(Seven
8	Eight	(Eight)
9	Nine	(Niner)
0	Zero	(Zero)

AVIATION VOCABULARY

AIM: Airman's Information Manual published by the government
AIR TRAFFIC CONTROL (ATC): An FAA service that provides safe and orderly flow of air traffic
AUX: Auxiliary
APU: Auxiliary Power Unit. An onboard electrical system that generates power
ATIS: Automatic Terminal Information Service. A continuous broadcast of information relating to terminal areas
BED & BREAKFAST: A room in a guest house that includes full breakfast
BELOW MINIMUMS: Weather conditions inadequate for aircraft to approach and land
CATERER: Food and beverage facility that provides service to aircraft
CEILING: Height above the earth's surface of the lowest layer of clouds or other phenomena
CFM: Confirm
CHG: Charge
CLEAR AIR TURBULENCE: Turbulence that occurs in clear air and is associated with wind shear
COLD FRONT: Cold air replacing warm air at the boundary of two air masses
CONF: Confirmed
CONNECTING ROOMS: 2 rooms connected with a door separate from the corridor
CONTINENTAL UNITED STATES: The 49 states of America plus the District of Columbia
CONTROL TOWER: Aviation center that guides planes in and out of its airport
CORPORATE RATE: A pre-arranged rate for services between provider and user
DAY RATE: Rate for use of day accommodation only. Does not cover overnight stay
DEADHEAD: (DHD). Operate a flight with no passengers
DE-ICING: Chemicals and water are sprayed over parts of plane to remove buildup of snow and ice
DEP: Depart
DEPARTURE TAX: Fee charge for individuals to enter or leave a city or country
DISP: Dispatch. Schedules and dispatches aircraft for flight
DOWNBURST: Intense downdraft of winds that cause severe damage near the ground
ETA: Estimated time of arrival
ETE: Estimated time en route
FAA: Federal Aviation Administration which governs aviation
FAR: Federal Aviation Regulations
FBO: Fixed Base Operator. Located at an air terminal and supplies services including maintenance and fuel, etc
FE: Flight Engineer
FINAL APPROACH: Final path of aircraft before landing on the runway
FLAMEOUT: Unexpected loss of engine power
FLT: Flight
FLIGHT PLAN: Detailed account of future trip giving route, altitude and anticipated times for flight
FYI: For your information
GALLEY: The aircraft kitchen
GMT: Greenwich Mean Time
GO AROUND: Instructions given to pilots advising them to abandon approach for landing
GRATUITIES: Tips or gifts given as extra payment for services rendered
GROUND PLANS/ARRANGEMENTS: Arrangements for anything on land – hotels, transport, meals
HANDLER: Person who supplies support service to an aircraft once landed
HEADING: Direction in which plane is pointing
HELIPAD/HELIPORT: Designated area for helicopter to take off and land
HLD: Hold

HOLDING PROCEDURE: Pilots of aircraft are instructed to remain in specified airspace until clearance received from Air Traffic Control

HOSPITALITY SUITE: Hotel room used for entertaining

HUMIDITY: Amount of water vapor in the air

HYPOXIA: Result of insufficient oxygen in the body

IFR: Instrument flight rules observed by pilots

IFR CONDITIONS: Weather or visibility below the minimums for visual flying

INCL: Include

INTL: International

ITINERARY: Detailed account of trip

JET STREAM: Concentrated high-speed winds at high altitude

KNOT: Measurement of speed. One unit equals one nautical mile (6,080 feet) per hour. (A land mile equals (5,280 feet)

LANDING GEAR: the nosewheel and two main wheels (or tailwheel) of an aircraft.

LAV: Lavatory, toilet

LEG: Individual part of a flight between takeoff and arrival

MANIFEST: The official document listing names of all on board an aircraft including animals and cargo

MAYDAY: Imminent danger requiring immediate assistance. Same as SOS

MISC.: Miscellaneous

MOTEL: Type of hotel where motorists can usually drive up to front door of their room or suite

MSG: Message

MSL: Mean Sea Level. The height above sea level

MURPHY BED: A bed that is contained in a wall unit and folds down when ready to use

N/A: Not available or not applicable

NTSB: National Transportation Safety Board

PAX: Passenger/s

PILOT IN COMMAND (PIC): The main pilot responsible for the entire operation and safety of the plane and passengers

PER DIEM: A daily rate or fee

PROOF OF CITIZENSHIP: A legal document that proves where a person was born – birth certificate

RES: Reservation or booking

RESERVATION: Prior arrangements made for use of room, transport, etc

RESORT: Vacation place that offers entertainment, recreation and usually accommodations

RON: Remain overnight. This means you will stay somewhere overnight

SECOND IN COMMAND (SIC): Refers to pilot below the pilot in command

SERVICE CHARGE: Extra fee applied to a bill as a replacement for tipping

STANDBY: Temporarily wait for a few minutes

STOPOVER: A short stop in a journey usually staying overnight

VALIDATE: Official proof that documents are in order – e.g., stamp a passport

VFR: Visual flight rules as observed by pilot

VIP: Very important person/passenger

VISA: A special permit in addition to a passport that allows a person to enter a country

WX: Weather

ZULU: Zulu Time. Also means Universal Coordinated Time (UTC)

AFTERWORD

It's an interesting paradox that some of the most famous people in the world who are sequestered behind security guards, bulletproof vehicles, and who are generally inaccessible personally to the world around them, can become as a result of your desire to serve, a part of your everyday life. For those of you who dare to pursue this career the rewards are unsurpassable. Color codes, cultural lines and societies' boundaries dissipate as you travel from one country to another, with distance and time dissolving into another reality. Gone will be the office politics, the freeway rush hour and the daily eight-to-five monotony, until termination or death do you part. The choice is yours.

In writing this book I have hoped to impart what I have learned so that you, too, could share the same joy I had in reaching beyond the believable, into a world of the absolutely incredible. When you do, be sure to write or e-mail me concerning your success in going, beyond the red carpet. God bless.

Gail Hopke, P.O. Box 12847, Palm Desert, CA 92255, USA. E-mail: kengail@earthlink.net

ABOUT THE AUTHOR

Gail Hopke considers herself a New Zealand born, Australian raised, American. Reared on a ranch in the outback of New Zealand she quickly realized that her family's love of the land was a far cry from her love of travel and international cultures. It would take years though for this dream to be realized, as she placed motherhood and education ahead of her career. Eventually, no matter what diploma she came home with, there was always the constant yearning of foreign lands and cultures beckoning her departure. As a trainee pilot she had a chance meeting with a captain who enlightened her regarding the incredible world of corporate aviation and thus a new dimension in her life began. Today she is retired from the ranks of flight attending, but says she still holds in awe the crews who fly the skies, along with her husband, her family, friends, the editor and publisher, and most of all, God.

Printed in the United States
32066LVS00001B/265